The Icky, Sticky and GROSS Fascinating FACTBOOK

Shar Levine and Leslie Johnstone

Mud Puddle Books
NEW YORK

SL – For my mall golfing partner Diane Osatuik,
who brings great joy, laughter and
cardio "exercise" into my life. Thanks.

LJ – For my friends Siobhan and Mabella and
their families. See you soon!

The Icky, Sticky and Gross Fascinating Factbook
by Shar Levine and Leslie Johnstone

© 2008 by Mud Puddle Books, Inc.

Published by
Mud Puddle Books, Inc.
54 W. 21st Street
Suite 601
New York, NY 10010
info@mudpuddlebooks.com

ISBN: 978-1-60311-145-4

Interior book design and photo research by Michelle Gengaro-Kokmen.

Complete photo credits on page 115

Printed in China

CONTENTS

INTRODUCTION

When you smell **barf** does it make you want to hurl? How would you react to a farting snake? Have you ever walked into a spider's web only to have to pry the sticky stuff off your face and hair? And did you know the ocean has **snot**? Have you decided that perhaps all this is too much information?

If you aren't faint of heart, then this is the book for you! If on the other hand you have a weak stomach and sensitive nature, you may wish to skip to the last page. Actually, don't worry. Nothing in this book will hurt you. If you have the courage to read each and every page of this book, you will be rewarded with enough bizarre information to disgust every member of your family during dinner. Now, with that in mind, be prepared to be totally grossed out.

Icky   **Sticky**   **Stinky**   **Gross**

Next to the title of each chapter is an icon that will tell you if the section is icky, sticky, stinky or gross. Some things are sticky or stinky or both at the same time. Icky and gross may be in the mind of the reader. You get to decide.

YOUR BODY

Everyone has a body, but do you know all the things that are going on in and around you? After reading this section you will have a better understanding of why your farts smell, how your body makes snot, and where the yellow stain on your t-shirt came from.

Vomit

The Chunder Down Under

Whether you say that you **throw up, hurl, puke, barf, up-chuck, toss your cookies** or **pray to the porcelain god,** what you mean is that you vomit. There are lots of ways to express how you've expressed yourself.

If you were in Australia you would say chunder. In England you might use a charming Cockney phrase **Wallace and Gromit** or even talking to **Ralph and Earl.** Some people **blow chunks, shout groceries, make street pizzas, sick up, keel** or **spew.**

We all know that sick feeling when you begin to salivate as the weird nauseating feeling hits your stomach and up comes breakfast, lunch, dinner or whatever you ate last.

Did You Know...

Ambergris

Your vomit may stink, but whale's vomit smells heavenly. **Ambergris,** an aged form of whale vomit, has a very gentle smell but it doesn't start out that way. When the whale excretes this lump of bile and waste it smells pretty vile. Over the course of about ten years it matures and the putrid smell disappears. The final product is valued because it is used to make perfumes and it can sell for over $20 a gram!

Having Breakfast Twice

That nasty stuff you see in the bowl after you lose your breakfast is basically the contents of your stomach. Vomit consists of slightly digested food, stomach acids, and slimy mucus. It can also contain bodily fluids such as **blood** and **bile**. Bile is a greenish liquid produced by your liver that you use to digest food. It isn't usually found in your stomach, but it can move into your stomach if you vomit a lot. Blood in vomit is never a good sign. No matter what is in your vomit it always smells absolutely disgusting!

Laugh 'Til You Puke

There are lots of reasons why people vomit. It can be due to a virus or a blockage in your digestive system. You could have motion sickness or a concussion. Women throw up when they are pregnant. People vomit when they have consumed too much alcohol or other drugs. Some people even lose their lunch when they are nervous, or when they laugh, cough or hiccup too much. Many different medical conditions can cause people to vomit. Reading this book might make you vomit because some people vomit when they see, hear or think about other people vomiting.

Gag Me, I Feel Retched

No matter what the cause, vomiting works in a predictable sequence. First, you feel nausea, that **queasy** feeling in the pit of your stomach. Then, your mouth waters as you begin to **salivate**. Sometimes you **retch** or **gag,** which is like vomiting where nothing comes out. At this point you may find that you are sweating or that your heart is beating rapidly. Finally the muscles in-

side your digestive tract work in reverse and your diaphragm and abdominal muscles tighten to force the partly digested food up into and out of your stomach. The vomit travels up your esophagus (the tube in your throat) and out your mouth and sometimes your nose. If you are lucky it ends up in a bowl or the toilet and not all over you or your friends.

What Goes Down Must Come Up

Vomiting, or emesis as it is called by the medical profession, can sometimes be a good thing. If you have eaten spoiled food it might be a good thing to have it removed from your stomach. Drugs called emetics that make you vomit are used as treatment when people swallow certain poisons. Not all poisons should be vomited; some can hurt your throat when they come back up.

MUCUS AND SNOT

'Snot What You Think It Is

It's slimy, it's nasty and it's running down the back of your throat! What is it? It's mucus.

Mucus is a slippery fluid that comes from body parts called mucus membranes. You have mucus membranes in a bunch of places in your body including your stomach, lungs, eyes, mouth, and your nose. **Snot** is the mucus made in your nose. Your snot, like most of your body, is primarily made up of water. Add in a few tears, some proteins and salts and you have a thick slimy mixture. You make snot all the time, about a cup or so each day, but most of the time you don't even notice it, as it just trickles down the back of your throat when you swallow.

Boogie on Down

Snot is good for you. It lines your nasal passages and helps trap bad stuff that is in the air you breathe. The little hairs in your nose are kept moist by the mucus that can trap the dirt and germs in the air. When the mucus is dirty it dries out and forms thicker dried lumps of snot and dirt. This is the stuff that you dig out when you pick your nose. Some people call these lumps **boogers, boogies** or **bogies** but whatever you call them, their presence means your nose is working properly.

I Have a Cold In My Nose

When you get a head cold one of the first things that happen is that your nose produces lots of clear mucus. With a bad cold you can produce more than ten times the normal amount. This is your body's way of repelling invaders by forcing out the germs that cause the cold. You can get rid of the excess snot by blowing your nose. Sometimes, if the cold continues, the mucus turns a **putrid yellow, green** or even **brown** due to bacteria or your body's response to a virus. Usually your body can cure the cold with lots of rest and fluids, but sometimes you need to take antibiotics to kick infections associated with the cold.

Come In From the Cold

Runny noses don't just happen from getting colds. Another way to get a runny nose is to go out in the cold. In the cold the little hairs called cilia in the back of your nose slow down. When this happens instead of going down your throat the snot comes dripping out your nose. Sometimes, if your nose gets really cold, the mucus becomes thicker and it only runs when you go inside and warm up. Some people get all snotty when they are around certain pollens. If you have hay fever you know that your nose can run like it's doing the Boston Marathon.

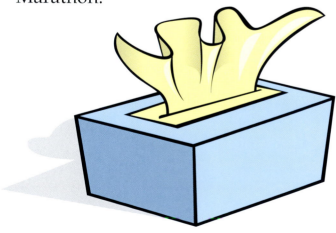

FECES

What Goes In Must Come Out

Everybody eats, so everybody has to poop. Poop or feces as it is more politely termed is the solid waste left over after your food has been digested.

It is a mixture of water, lots of bacteria, fiber, undigested food, bile salts and bilirubin. Bilirubin is a yellowish brown chemical produced by the liver when it breaks down your old red blood cells. Feces are usually covered in a slimy mucus coating that allows your poop to move through your digestive system and exit your anus.

Oh Crap!

If you have ever eaten a whole plateful of beets you may know that poop can be different colors. Babies start out with a very sticky **greenish** type of poop called meconium. Then their poop becomes yellowish and finally brown when they start eating different types of food. Food coloring can make your poop colored if you eat a lot of artificially colored food or drinks. So can certain foods, like beets. Certain medical conditions can make your feces range in color from white to black. Mostly though, poop is yellowy brown due to the presence of **bilirubin.**

And a One and a Two

Certain foods you eat don't get digested very well. That's why you may see corn kernels in your poop. You may also see certain seeds or nuts or even beans when you do number two. Sometimes feces sink in the toilet bowl and sometimes they float. The floaters are caused by the stool being less dense than the water, either because of trapped gases in the feces or due to a higher fat content in the undigested food that makes up the stool.

What is That Nasty Smell?

Let's face it – poop stinks. Poop contains several different chemicals that have very nasty odors. These chemicals are made in your digestive system by the bac-

teria that help digest your food. Chemicals such as hydrogen sulphide gas, indole and skatole smell really disgusting. Hydrogen sulphide gas smells like rotten eggs. Indole and skatole smell like feces, but strangely enough, in very small amounts they have nice floral scents and are used to make perfumes.

Mmm....Tasty

Of course, there are animals that eat poop, so they must not mind the smell. Small micro-organisms such as bacteria eat poop, and so do some insects like the dung beetle. People also eat poop, but usually not on purpose. If someone handles food after a trip to the bathroom without washing

Dung beetle and dinner.

his hands, the food may have small amounts of poop on it. Or poop can enter the water supply when someone disposes of her feces in a way that contaminates the water. There are lots of diseases spread this way, from pinworms to cholera and typhus. So your mother was right when she said to always wash your hands after going to the bathroom!

Running on Empty

When your food goes through your digestive system one of the last places it gets to is your colon. The **gloppy poop** in your colon dries out as water passes through the lining of your colon. This solidifies your feces so you can poop it out. If the water doesn't get absorbed, your feces stays watery and you have diarrhea.

Several different culprits can cause diarrhea, from a touch of stomach flu to something you ate or drank. In developing countries the cause is often unsanitary drinking water. There are also many different medical conditions that can cause you to have the runs.

Diarrhea is no fun, and for children in developing countries it is potentially fatal. In the late 1970s doctors realized that many children were dying from diarrhea simply because they became dehydrated. A group of doctors developed a simple, inexpensive drink that could be given to these children. This drink contained sugars and salts that replenished those lost in the diarrhea. Very quickly the number of recorded deaths decreased by more than two-thirds. This very successful treatment, called oral rehydration therapy, has been distributed by UNICEF and the World Health Organization.

Urinalysis Is As Good As Mine

Just as everybody poops if they eat, everybody that drinks has to **pee**. Your urine comes originally from your blood.

When your blood goes through your kidneys (which are two small organs in your abdomen located in the area of the small of your back) the waste products are filtered out and turned into pee.

Every day you pee an average of about 5 cups of urine. This yellowy to amber colored liquid is mostly water with some salts and other chemicals called urea, uric acid and creatinine. Urine can also include small amounts of sugars and proteins, as well as other chemicals that the person has ingested or produced in their body.

Water....I Need Water!

If you become stranded in the desert or somewhere there is no water, should you drink your pee? Because urine has a high concentration of salt, drinking your own pee will, in the long run, make you more dehydrated than if you drank water. If you could evaporate the water from the pee and collect it in a plastic bag, it would be fine to drink that water, and it could save your life.

Multicolored Pee

Although pee is normally a clear yellow or yellowish amber color because of a chemical in pee called **urochrome,** there are lots of things that can make pee a different color. Certain vitamins and minerals taken in large amounts can make the pee green. Eating lots of beets, blackberries or rhubarb can make your pee reddish. Some medications or vitamins can make your pee orange. There are some medical conditions that cause pee to be brown or even black.

Stinky Pee

Certain foods you eat can change the smell of your pee. Coffee and asparagus are particularly known for making your urine smell funky. Not everyone makes smelly urine when they eat asparagus. It's an inherited trait, so, if you do, you probably take after your mom or dad. Even if asparagus does make your pee smell funny, you might

not know. The ability to smell the stinky asparagus smell is also an inherited one.

Water the Plants

Urea, found in urine, is a terrific source of the element nitrogen which can be used by plants. Of course, you shouldn't go and pee on your houseplants as your urine is too concentrated for the plants and would likely kill them. In many countries organic gardeners are now examining ways to use human pee as a safe and inexpensive fertilizer.

Whizzy Woad

Stale urine, urine that has been sitting around awhile, contains ammonia. The ammonia is made by bacteria that enters the pee from the air, breaking down the **urea** and **uric acid.** Stale urine has been used since the days of the Romans to treat wool before dyeing. In parts of Scotland every farm had a barrel of **old pee** where the wool would be dipped to clean off the natural oils. One of the dyes used was a blue dye called **woad,** which was made by fermenting leaves of a plant with stale urine.

There's Gold In Them There Urinals

Early alchemists thought that urine contained gold. This is probably due to the lovely yellow color. Alas, there is no gold in urine, but in 1669, a German alchemist named Henning Brandt discovered phosphorus in urine while he was attempting to extract gold. Today phosphorus is used to make matches, detergent and fertilizers, but in Brandt's time, there wasn't much practical use for phosphorus. Consequently, Brandt didn't do much with his accidental discovery. Actually, back then, phosphorus was a difficult substance to handle. If it isn't stored under water, phosphorus can spontaneously ignite.

Flatulence

Gassy Jack

Let's face it, farting is embarrassing. But we all do it. In fact we do it about ten times a day on average. When excess **gas** builds up in your digestive system it has to find a way out. You can either **belch** or you can **fart.** Passing gas is nature's way of helping you get rid of the gas.

There are two main ways that gas builds up inside your gut. One is when you swallow air, which can happen when you eat or drink too fast, when you chew gum or even when you drink soda pop. The other way is when you produce gas from foods you eat.

The More You Eat, The More You Toot

Some foods you eat are thought to be particularly fart-producing. These include beans (some-times called the magical fruit), cabbage, broccoli, asparagus, Brussels sprouts and onions. In addition, some people find that starchy food, like crackers or po-

tatoes, cause them to toot. Other people, who have difficulty digesting milk sugar or lactose, get gassy when they drink milk or eat cheese.

Silent but Deadly

Some people make **really smelly** farts while others have farts that hardly **stink** at all. Farts are made up of several gases. There is nitrogen and oxygen gas from the air as well as hydrogen, carbon dioxide and methane gas that are produced during digestion. These gases don't have an odor. The stinky gases are small amounts of the same gases found in feces: indole and skatole as well as sulphur containing gases like hydrogen sulphide gas.

The Fartiste

Farts are sometimes called toots because of the noise they make, and one man made such musical toots that he was able to make a good living farting nightly on stage. Joseph Pugol, who had the nickname **Le Petomane** (which translated means **the Fartiste**), was a French entertainer who performed at the Moulin Rouge in Paris in the late 1800s. He had an entire act built around his ability to fart creatively on demand. This act did so well that he was able to support his wife and ten children on the proceeds of his musical tooting. This tradition continues today with a modern day **Fartiste** named Paul Oldfield. He lives in England where he performs at comedy festivals using the name **Mr. Methane.**

SWEAT
and Body Odor

Stinky Pits

Lift up your arm and smell your pit. If you're still a little kid, this area many not gross you out. However, if you have hairs springing from here, you may be met with a whiff of **eau d' pew.**

Because You're Hot

Sweat is a mixture of water, salt, and small amounts of other chemicals that come out of your sweat **glands.** Your body has between 2.5 and 4 million sweat glands, but it is the **apocrine** glands under your arms that release the stinkiest sweat. You only develop these glands at puberty, so little kids don't have stinky sweat. Bacteria on your skin like the small amounts of fatty material in this perspira-

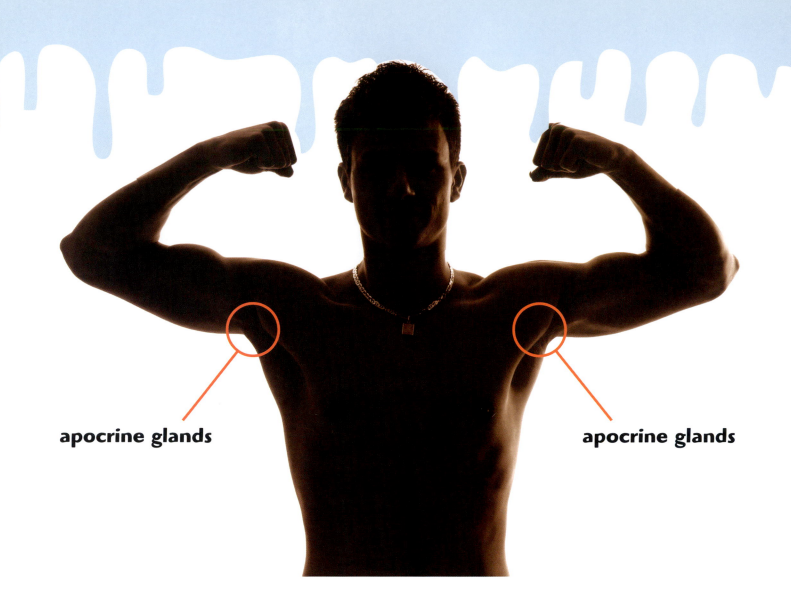

apocrine glands

apocrine glands

tion the best. Your sweat itself doesn't actually have much of an odor, it's those pesky bacteria eating your sweat that give off the stinky smells. The more you sweat, the more the bacteria grow and you could be harboring a whole colony.

During hot weather or when you exercise, you perspire so that you will cool down. When the sweat on your skin evaporates you will feel cooler. To see how this works try spritzing yourself with some water the next time you are outside on a hot day. Doesn't it feel cooler now?

If you get too hot, you could develop a condition called **hyperthermia**. If your temperature continues to rise, you run the risk of a heat stroke, which is very dangerous. On a hot day. if you become dizzy or confused, make sure you get cooled off right away.

Technicolor sweat

If you think that your sweat is gross, be happy it isn't worse.

Most people have colorless sweat, but if you have **chromhidrosis** you could have sweat that is yellow, green, blue or even black. This is caused by a normal body chemical called **lipofuscin** that a few people have a lot of in their sweat.

If you have pink sweat you would be a hippopotamus. When hippos get hot, they secrete a pinkish colored sweat. Hippos don't necessarily want to wash this off as it serves as a kind of sunscreen. Don't know if it's an SPF 30 or 45, but it is, no doubt, waterproof.

Belly Buttons
and belly button lint

Navel Gazing

If you were born, you have a belly button or navel as they are sometimes called. Your belly button is what you're left with after the stump of your umbilical cord dries out and falls off.

What is an umbilical cord? It's the tube that connects babies to their mothers so that babies can be supplied with nutrients before they are born. Which type of belly button you have is a matter of chance, but it is more common for people to have **innies** than **outies**.

Belly Button Lint

If your belly button is an innie, you may discover that tiny fibers and hairs can lodge there. Belly button lint is the fluffy stuff that accumulates in your belly button in between baths and showers. A physicist named Dr. Karl Kruszelnicki researched belly button lint and found that that men produce more lint than women and people with more hair around their belly buttons produced the most lint. The most common color for belly button lint is blue, perhaps because more people wear blue clothing than other colors.

A Guinness Gut

No matter how weird, if there is a world record for it, the Guinness Book of World Records will have it. The world's largest collection of belly button lint from a single person belongs to an Australian gentleman by the name of Graham Barker. He collected his lint daily for more than 20 years!

Earwax

Polishing Your Ears

Earwax is found in your ears, but it isn't really wax. It's the waxy stuff secreted by cerumen glands in your ear canal. Technically called cerumen, this yellowy stuff helps keep your inner ears clean and lubricated.

Any little fleck of dust or garbage that makes its way into your ear canal will get stuck in the sticky cerumen, just like a fly on flypaper. The wax eventually makes its way to the surface where you may rub it out of your ear with your finger. Don't taste it…it tastes very bitter and yucky.

blocked with earwax you should see a doctor. Using swabs to clean your ears can be dangerous and cause hearing problems.

Tiny Elbows

You may have heard it said that you should never put anything into your ear smaller than your elbow. This is a good saying, as it is not a good idea to put stuff in your ears. If your ears become

Hairy Ears

The Guinness World Record holder for having the longest ear hair is Radhakant Bajpai of India. In May 2003 his ear hair was found to be more than 5 inches long.

Bad Breath

Halitosis

Stick out your tongue. You might think that your tongue is smooth but it actually has lots of bumps and crevices where tiny bacteria and germs can hide.

Just as they do in lots of other places in and on your body, the bacteria on your tongue can make chemicals that stink. These sulphur containing chemicals smell really nasty. It isn't just the bacteria on your tongue, but also the ones on other parts of your mouth and around the base of your teeth that make these odoriferous chemicals. If you keep your mouth clean through brushing and flossing your breath will be sweet smelling. Don't forget to brush your tongue and cheeks while cleaning your teeth! Oh, **halitosis** is the high-falutin' word for bad breath.

Something Smells Fishy

Not only do bacteria in your mouth give you bad breath, but certain medical conditions can affect your breath as well. Some metabolic disorders can make your breath smell like nail polish remover, others can give your breath a smell like dead fish.

Malodorous Mouths

If you are planning to eat garlic or onions make sure to bring some mouthwash and a toothbrush. Both these foods are well known for giving people stinky breath. Other foods that can cause your mouth to smell are some types of fish and diets high in meat and fat.

SALIVA AND PHLEGM

Spit Balls

When you **spit,** you mostly spit out two different fluids, **saliva** and **phlegm.** Phlegm is the slippery sticky mucus in the parts of your respiratory system other than your nose.

Just like snot, phlegm is mainly made up of water, some proteins and salts. If you are healthy your phlegm is usually clear or white; if it is green, brown or yellow that can either be a sign that you are ill or a sign that you have been breathing in nasty stuff like cigarette smoke. Phlegm is useful as your respiratory system uses it to trap airborne particles so that they don't enter your lungs. Instead, you cough up the phlegm and either spit it out or swallow it.

Saliva, a fluid that is mostly water, is produced by the salivary glands, which are only found in your mouth. This fluid also contains a small amount of salts and proteins including some called **enzymes.**

Powerful Enzyme Action

Enzymes in your saliva start breaking down the food you eat, even while it is still in your mouth. If you don't believe this try this experiment. Put a soda cracker in your mouth and chew it without swallowing. At first it tastes salty from the salt on the cracker, but if you keep chewing long enough, the starch in the cracker is broken down by an enzyme called **amylase.** Amylase makes sugar and the cracker starts to taste sweet. This fast action helps protect your teeth because the enzymes in your saliva break down the food caught in your teeth so it doesn't cause decay.

Hucktoooey

You have lots of bacteria in your saliva; some scientists estimate as many as 700 different kinds, but antibacterial compounds in the saliva keep them under control. Because of this, it's unlikely that biting your lip will give you an infection. On the other hand, if someone cuts their knuckles on your teeth, their hand could easily become infected by the mouth bacteria. And you don't want to know what would happen to you if you were nibbled on by certain reptiles, like the komodo dragon. Now that's saliva with a real bite.

It's a good thing that people's

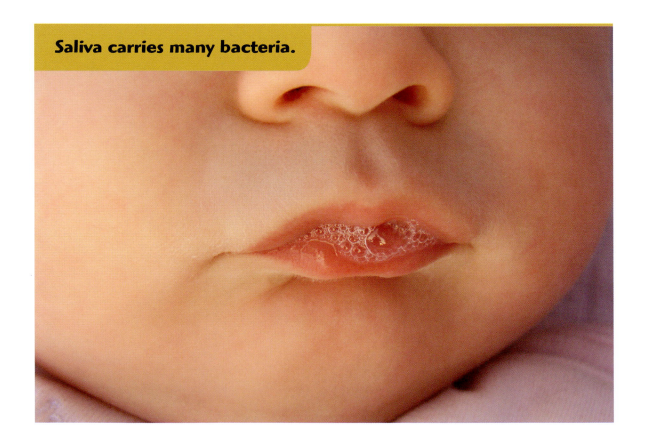

Saliva carries many bacteria.

saliva isn't toxic. When people kiss they sometimes share some spit. While the saliva won't kill you, it can spread some diseases like **colds, the flu** and **mononucleosis,** which used to be called the **kissing disease.** Although mono is contagious, you don't have to kiss someone to get it.

Don't Drool on the Da Vinci

You should never spit on art work, but, art conservators (people who clean and restore paintings) do it all the time. They use cotton swabs soaked in saliva to clean old and precious artwork. Saliva has the right combination of enzymes, water and other mild chemicals to make the paintings sparkle without stripping away the paint. Fortunately you make a fair amount of saliva in a day, about 3 cups full, so there will be lots to make the swabs nice and juicy.

You Can Call Me Pavlov's dog

Think about a nice warm slice of rich creamy chocolate cake. Or

crispy carrot sticks. Or something else you like to eat. Do you start to drool? Your brain can make you begin to salivate. This is because thinking about food, or smelling food, or tasting food triggers your brain in a process called **parasympathetic stimulation** and signals are sent to your salivary glands. This was first demonstrated by a Russian scientist named Ivan Pavlov who showed that dogs fed after hearing a ringing bell would salivate whenever they heard the bell.

Teeth

Calling All Tooth Fairies

When you are six or seven losing a tooth is a cause for rejoicing. Many children are delighted to wake up to find cold hard cash under their pillows as a reward for losing a tooth.

Tooth loss later in life is not a very good thing. In fact, it's a bit gross. How do teeth get lost and, more to the point, how can you stop it from happening? It is all about brushing and flossing.

Spelunking in Your Mouth

Have you ever had a **cavity**? Dental caries—the crumbling and decaying of teeth also known as cavities or **tooth decay**—is very common. In fact, it is the most common medical condition people have after the common cold. Left untreated, it will lead to huge caves or caverns in you teeth. These caverns are carved out by the action of your mouth bacteria. The bacteria eat carbohydrates, which are sugars and starches. They make acids and the acids eat away at the enamel of your teeth. Once the acids eat through the enamel, they attack the bony tissue underneath. This bony tissue is called **dentin.** Without the protection of enamel, the tooth soon has a big hole in it.

Having a cavity can be very painful. If the cavity is deep into the tooth, part of the root may be exposed. If this happens, eating hot, cold or sweet foods can hurt so much that it might cause you to scream.

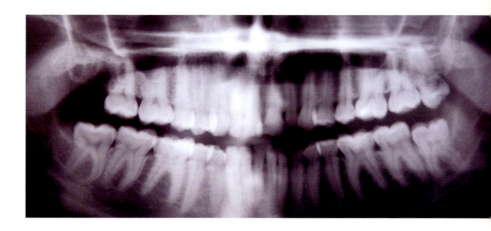

Gross Gums

You might think that **gum disease** is only for old folks, but problems with your gums can happen at any age. If your gums are not healthy you can get bad breath, bleeding gums and even lose your teeth. A doctor who studies gum or **periodontal** disease is a **periodontist,** a special kind of dentist. Nasty gums begin with plaque, a sticky

bunch of bacteria that attach to your teeth. The bacteria give off sticky stinky and irritating chemicals that can damage your gum tissue, your teeth, and even the bones in your jaw. Fortunately you can remove the plaque any time you want by brushing and flossing your teeth. So brush and floss every day.

Invasion

Gum disease starts with **gingivitis,** an inflammation or swelling and reddening of the gums. If your gums bleed when you brush or floss you probably have this condition. A healthy diet, reducing sugars and starches, and regular brushing should take care of this. Visiting a dentist for a cleaning is also a good choice. The bacteria in your mouth live on sugars and starches, so the less you feed them, the less they will grow out of control. You really don't need bacteria taking over your mouth…so take control!

Abscess Makes the Heart Grow Fonder

If you have ever had a toothache you know that it is nasty. An even worse toothache is one caused by an **abscess.** This is where a pool of pus forms in the middle of your tooth. Sometimes this happens because of tooth decay, but it can also happen if your tooth is injured. The pus is a mixture

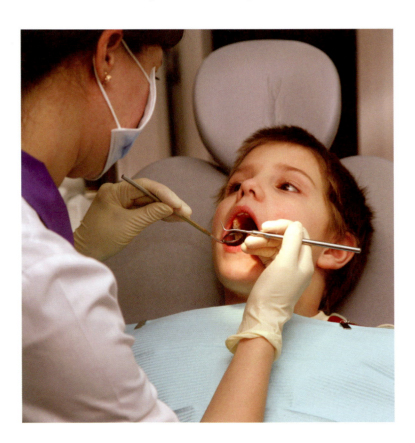

of living and dead bacteria, dead tissue from your gums and tooth and also your white blood cells that move into the tooth area to fight the infection. Dentists treat this condition with antibiotics and sometimes with surgery. The sooner abscesses are treated the easier they are to treat and the less likely the abscess is to spread to places like your brain, heart and lungs.

You Are Very Wise

If your teeth don't pop up through your gums like they are supposed to, they are called **impacted** teeth. Many people have impacted teeth and usually they are no problem. Lots of people have impacted wisdom teeth, which are the last set of teeth to emerge, usually in your late teens or early twenties. And no, having these teeth doesn't make you any wiser! Impacted wisdom teeth can cause your other teeth to become twisted or displaced, and, if are only partially impacted, they can be hard to keep clean. If this happens you will probably have to have them removed.

Feet

Don't Spread This On Toast

When you take off your socks at the end of day do you notice that you have accumulated some crud between your toes? This is **toe jam.**

It's a mixture of fibers from your socks, dead skin cells and bacterial leftovers. You probably notice it mostly in the winter when you are more likely to have your little piggies trapped in socks and shoes all day. Of course, if you had more webbing between your toes, you may not swim better but you would find that you trapped less toe jam.

Why Do Your Feet Smell and Your Nose Runs?

Your feet have about a quarter of a million sweat glands. So do your hands. So why is it that your feet stink but your hands don't? It turns out that the culprit for stinky feet is sweat. Your hands aren't usually sweaty and damp for long periods of time. It is the sweat that sticks around in your socks and shoes that gives your feet that funky odor. Sweat by itself doesn't stink, but if you feed it to the bacteria that live on your skin they can change sweat into **eau de pew**! Skin bacteria love a warm damp spot and they also love to dine on your dead skin and the oils on your skin. Especially stinky feet can be caused by a skin bacterium called **micrococcus sendentarius.** The stinkiest feet smell like rotten eggs due to the sulphur containing chemicals excreted by skin bacteria.

Sweet Smelling

At traditional Japanese restaurants, you are asked to remove your shoes before you enter tatami rooms (rooms covered with thick straw mats). It would be terribly embarrassing to be banned from dining because of smelly feet. Here's how to keep your feet smelling sweetly, or at least not smelling awful.

Change your socks and shoes often. Keep your feet dry. Make sure your socks are washed and your shoes too, if they can be. You might take shoes that can't be washed to your local bowling alley to ask if they will use their ultraviolet lights to disinfect them or if they can recommend a disinfecting spray.

Cheesy Feet

Mmmm tasty…if you were going to choose a snack you probably wouldn't chow down on something that smelled like sweaty feet. That is unless you were a malaria mosquito. Dutch researchers found that given a choice between

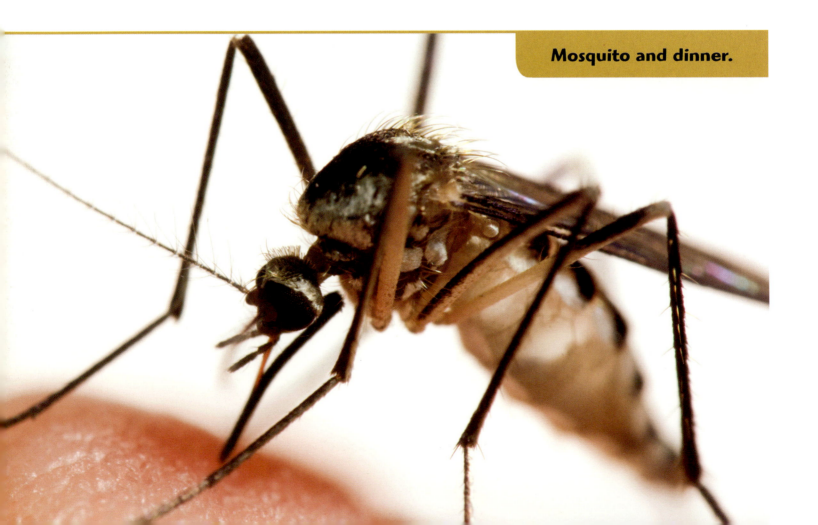

Mosquito and dinner.

clean and stinky unwashed feet, these **mozzies** (mosquitoes) over-whelmingly prefer the sweaty funky ones. Not only do they pre-fer **eau de toe cheese,** they also like the scent of a stinky white cheese called Limburger. This cheese has the aroma of sweaty feet and could one day be used to trap mosquitoes.

Arm Chair Athletes

You don't have to be a jock to get **athlete's foot.** This nasty fun-gal infection can attack your feet even if the only tennis you play is a video game. Itchy feet and toes or feet that sting and seem ten-der are all signs that you might have athlete's foot. This is caused by a fungus that grows in the nice damp, warm areas between your toes. This fungus belongs to a group called **dermatophytes.** These are the same types of fungi that cause ringworm, which isn't a worm but was given its name before people learned it was a fungus. To treat athlete's foot you can use an anti-fungal cream or powder and make sure you keep your feet clean and dry. And

don't share shoes: these fungi will spread to other people easily. If you like bowling, make sure the alley disinfects their rental footwear.

Pedi-cures

You will not want to wear open-toed shoes if your toenails are thick, yellow or brown and pro-viding a home for a **toenail fun-gus.** These fungi, like the ones that cause athletes feet, love the warmth and dampness of your feet. Your toenails give them a protective topping to hide under and the fungi will grow and even-tually destroy your nail. Tight shoes, toenail polish and damp feet all make this worse.

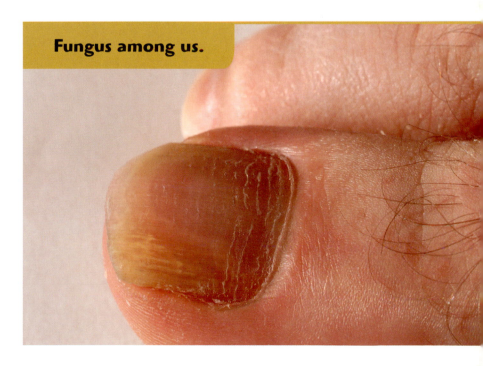

Fungus among us.

You Are So Flaky

If every time you wear black you notice white dots covering your shoulders you may have **dandruff.** The white stuff is flaked off skin plus, perhaps, some bacteria and fungus.

Dandruff, or **scurf** as it is sometimes called, can have several causes, from naturally dry skin to an infection of fungus. Skin cells live for about a month, but, when you have dandruff, the cells may only last for a few days. Sometimes people get dandruff when the weather changes or when they try a new shampoo. Luckily for you, it's not a dangerous condition, doesn't cause your hair to fall out and is fairly normal and common. Unluckily, you will have to brush or wash your black clothes to get them clean.

Babies and infants get a type of dandruff called **cradle cap.** It doesn't seem to bother them, but it can cover their entire scalp.

A Fungus Among Us

In some people, dandruff and other skin conditions such as **seborrheic dermatitis, eczema** and **psoriasis** may be connected by a tiny yeast-like fungus called

Malassezia globosa. This fungus lives all over you and eats small amounts of the oils secreted by your skin. One particularly oily spot on your skin is your scalp, so that is prime real estate for this little blob. Scientists have recently mapped the DNA of this fungus and hope to use this information to prepare treatments for some of these skin conditions. In addition, they hope the DNA mapping will provide insights in areas as varied as agriculture and human health.

Zits

It never fails. Any time you have an important event in your life you will be sure to have an important pimple. **Acne** is icky. Thousands of **pus-filled blobs** seem to take over your life as they take over your face. The sebaceous glands in your skin give off oil and when they work properly, the oil protects your face from wind and rain. When the glands overproduce oil it causes problems. The pores that the oil is released through become plugged. The extra trapped oil feeds the acne bacteria (Propionibacterium acnes) which irritates your skin. This irritation then causes your body to produce pus. Get enough inflammation and it can cause larger lumps and even thick scarring.

The exact causes of acne aren't completely understood, but several things can make it worse. Cosmetics, hairspray, sweating, stress and sports helmets and pads can all cause worse acne. So can certain drugs. Cleaning and scrubbing your skin can irritate the acne once you have it and picking or popping those **zits** can

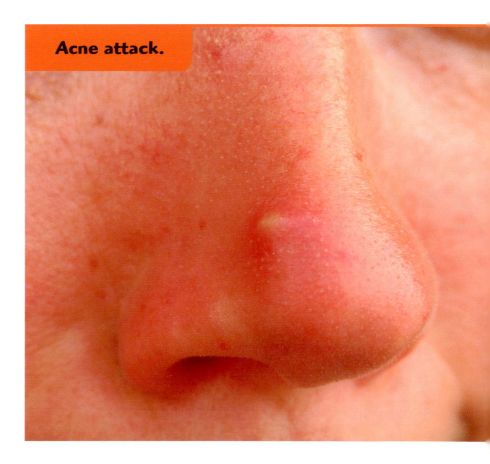

Acne attack.

give you scars. The good news is that eventually most people out grow the worst of the acne, and there are plenty of medical treatments that can be used until that happens.

Don't Kiss That Frog

You may have heard the story of the Frog Prince, where an enchanted frog is changed into a prince when kissed by a princess. You may have also heard that kissing frogs gives you **warts.** Both of these are fiction. Frogs don't give you warts any more than they will turn into princes if you kiss them. It should be noted that many women would risk warts if they knew kissing a frog would get them a prince.

Warts are very contagious, but you get them from people, not

Did You Know...

Duct tape therapy

One of the ways to treat warts is to use an over the counter treatment containing a chemical called salicylic acid. Another way is to cover the wart with duct tape. Sometimes doctors recommend using these treatments together. The acid and the duct tape irritate the warts and your body responds and heals, getting rid of the wart.

from amphibians. They are so contagious that if you have warts you should treat them immediately to avoid passing them on to your family and friends. The viruses that cause warts are called **papillomaviruses** and there are more than 100 types. Warts can grow anywhere on your body.

Burning Man

Ah…the joys of an afternoon spent at the beach. That is, until suppertime when you discover that all your exposed skin is beginning to hurt. **Redness, swelling, itching** and **blisters** filling with clear fluid make that lovely afternoon a sad memory. Finally, over the next few days, the redness goes and your skin begins to peel until you look like you are covered with tiny flakes of white plastic. Ah…summer.

Sunburns are caused by ultraviolet radiation coming from…you guessed it…the sun. If you have very fair skin, you will probably know what a sunburn is like. If you have darker skin the extra melanin (dark skin pigment) in your skin protects you from the sun's radiation. You can get a sunburn in as little as 10 or 15 minutes, but you may not realize you are burnt until a few hours later. Sunscreens can protect you from the sun's rays, but you will need to apply lots and reapply them often on very sunny days.

Sunburns aren't just painful, they are also dangerous. They can change the DNA, or genetic material, in the affected skin cells and this can lead to an increased risk of skin cancer as you get older.

Pus and Boots

Did you know that pus is actually good for you? It's your body's way of repelling invading bacteria. Numerous bacteria live in

Did You Know...

A layer of gas in the atmosphere containing a chemical called **ozone,** which is a type of oxygen gas, protects the Earth from the ultra-violet radiation of the sun. This layer is gradually being broken down by synthetic chemicals released into the atmosphere. The release of these chemicals has been reduced through the cooperation of many countries signing the Montreal Protocol in the late 1980s.

and on your body every day and they are mostly harmless. But sometimes these bacteria end up in the wrong place, like when skin bacteria gets into a cut, and you need to fight them off. How does this battle proceed? First, special cells in your body called **macrophages** sense tissue damage caused by the invading bacteria and send out a chemical alarm to call in other troops. Then the storm troopers, white blood cells called neutrophils, come in. The **neutrophils** completely surround the bacteria in a process called **phagocytosis.** Once the bactera are surrounded, the neutrophils eat them up and digest them. After the battle, the neutrophils die and the mixture of dead neutrophils, dead bacteria and a fluid high in proteins becomes pus.

EYE SPY

Mister Sandman

What do watery eyes and rhubarb have in common? Not a whole lot except that scientists call both of them **rheum.**

The eye kind of rheum is sometimes called sleep, as it often dries out and forms a crunchy crust when you are sleeping. This crust is made from dried tears, mucus and other body fluids as well as dead skin cells and dust. Legend has it that a fictional character called the Sandman sprinkles dust and sand into your eyes at night, causing the crust. That isn't what actually happens. These things don't just descend upon you at night, they are always in your eyes, but during the day you re-move them by blinking. A bit of crust in your eyes in the morning is normal, but if there is pus or a lot of crust, it may be a sign of an eye infection.

Pretty in Pink

If you have itchy red eyes, it might not be because you stayed up all night reading this book. You might have pink eye. **Pinkeye** isn't as pretty as it sounds. It is an eye infection involving the part of your eye called the **conjunctiva.**

This is the membrane that lines your eyelid and the area around your eyeball. Pinkeye is very common and often goes away on its own. However, it can be very contagious, so, if you think you have it, see your doctor. Most pinkeye is caused by viruses. You can help protect yourself by frequently washing your hands, not sharing facecloths and avoiding touching your eyes.

Eye Sty

Eye spy with my little eye something red and pussy. **Styes** are like pimples at the base of an eyelash. They are usually caused by bacteria called **Staphylococcus aureus,** sometimes called staph. The staph infection forms along the edge of the eyelid. Sometimes styes form near the tear ducts at the inside corner of the eye, but they can also be in the middle area of the eyelid. The infection starts out with a bit of tenderness. As the sty grows larger, it forms a head of pus. Eventually the sty pops and the pus drains out.

They Live Among Us

Ring Around the Rosy

When is a worm not a worm? When it is a **ringworm.** Ringworm is actually a fungal infection – that's right, a fungus like yeasts and mushrooms.

This condition was given its name due to the mistaken belief that the rings of itchy red skin were caused by a worm making its way in circles under your skin. As the fungus grows under your skin it leaves a clear section in the middle and comes to the surface at the outside of the ring. These rings can show up anywhere on your body--even in your hair, which can fall out in the area around the ring. Mushrooms in the forest sometimes grow in this same way and are called **fairy rings.**

Ringworm is contagious and can be passed on by sharing combs, hats or clothing. The infection can also be spread by skin to skin contact, so if you have ringworm, you probably want to take a break from wrestling. Ringworm is a **zoonotic** disease which means it can pass between animals and humans. You can even get ringworm from your family pets, especially cats and cows (if you have a family cow). Fortunately this condition is—usually—completely reversible with anti-fungal treatment.

Head Pets

Even if you have never been able

to have a cat or dog, you may have had pets: **head pets.** These are little creatures who love to live in your hair. **Lice** are tiny brownish-grey insects that live on people's heads. They drink small amounts of blood that they get by biting the skin on your scalp or neck. This tends to irritate your skin and make it itchy. This usually gets the lice noticed. Once you're aware of these little parasites, it's easy to kill them with an insecticide. But that doesn't completely get rid of the lice because they leave their eggs behind. Lice eggs, called **nits,** are tiny little grains that the female

louse lays on your scalp. The eggs become attached to your hair so that they don't shake loose. It can take about a week for all the lice to hatch, so you will need several treatments to make sure they are all gone. While you wait for the lice to hatch it is good to comb out the eggs with a very fine-tooth comb. The eggs can also be attached to your hats, your hairbrush, your comb, your towels and your bedding. A trip through a hot washer and drier usually gets rid of them.

Mighty Mite

They are so tiny you can't see them. They dig their way into your skin, and they can live in your bed. What are they? **Mites.** The mites that cause a skin condition called **scabies** are called **Sarcoptes scabei.** You can easily pick them up if you come into contact with someone who has an infestation of these tiny creatures. Watch out! You don't even need to touch the other person. These creatures are great jumpers. They'll be happy to change hosts if you come into contact with infected clothing, towels

Head louse

Did You Know...

Flea

Tick

Living creatures are sometimes called organisms. They can look after themselves or they can be **parasites.** A parasite is a creature that gets its food and protection by living in or on another organism called a **host.** Parasites can move between animals and people, or between different people, or even between animals. They are often the causes of diseases but even those that don't cause disease still disadvantage their hosts.

Leeches

or bedding. Once the mite is on board, it burrows in and, after a few days, you become super itchy due to an allergic reaction. Doctors treat scabies with a skin cream.

There are many different types of mites and not all of them cause scabies. Mites are not insects. They are related to spiders. Like spiders they have eight legs. Most types are harmless to you. You don't notice the different mites around you because they are too small to see without a microscope, but they are found in large numbers in, for example, house dust.

Incredible Journey

Inch by Inch

One morning you wake up and there is a reddish lump on your leg. A few days or hours later a blister appears, and then it bursts.

You climb into the bathtub for a soak and happen to glance down at your leg. Sticking out of the hole in the center of the blister is a tiny worm head. This is what happens if you are a host to the **Guinea worm.** This worm, called **Dracunculus medinensis,** is a type of roundworm. Roundworms are tube-shaped and tapered at each end. They look like wriggling threads. About 50 different types of these worms infect humans. The usual treatment for Guinea worm is to pull the worm gently from the hole by winding it around a stick. This can take days or weeks depending on the size of the worm. Some of these worms can be almost three feet in length, so winding them out takes a while.

How do these worms get inside you? They have two hosts: people and a tiny **water flea.** The water flea eats up a juvenile form of the worm which is released when people with the worm go into the water. Then, the worm develops inside the water flea. If you drink water containing these fleas the worm starts to develop inside of you. About one year after you drank the water the worm works its way to the surface of your skin.

It is easy to stop yourself from swallowing the water fleas: just drink filtered water. Health organizations such as the Carter Center have been providing expertise and filtering materials to areas with infestations, and they hope to be able to eradicate Guinea worm worldwide.

Eye See You

One type of round worm you don't want to meet is the **loa loa worm.** These little creatures are also called the African **eyeworm** for reasons that will become obvious. If you are in West Africa and are bitten by a tiny fly, you may have taken on passengers – loa loa larva. The larva enter your body through the bite wound and take up residence under your skin. The worms live under your skin, but occasionally they decide to take a stroll and travel across the surface of your eye.

Water fleas

This visit to the surface of the eyeball is often what causes people to realize that they have become a host for this worm. Adult worms make lots of tiny threads called **microfilariae** that move from the lungs where they are found at night to the veins under the skin during the daytime.

When another tiny fly comes along to take a bite, it can scoop up some of these fibers. Inside the insect, the fibers develop into larvae that can be transferred to a new human host.

Break the Five Second Rule

The most common type of roundworm infection in the world is **ascariasis** caused by the **Ascaris lumbricoides** worm. This worm has eggs that are found in dirt, particularly dirt that may contain small

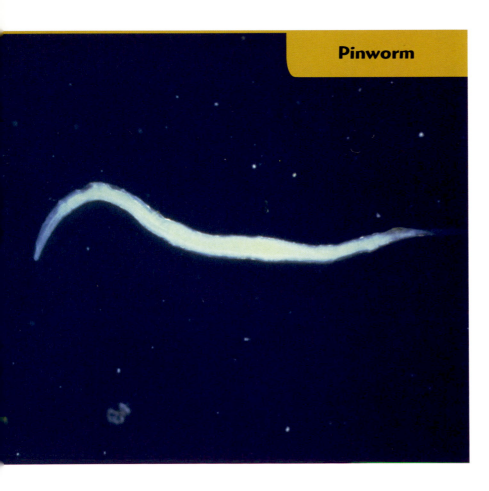

Pinworm

amounts of human feces. Typically the dirt is found on food that hasn't been washed or on food that has dropped on the floor and eaten without washing. Once you ingest the eggs they travel to your digestive system where they hatch. The baby worms work their way into your bloodstream and into your lungs. This is the gross part…you then cough up the worm larvae and swallow them. Once the worms are back in your digestive system they settle in your intestines where they eat what you eat. Worms in your intestines can grow to be over one foot in length! The females release eggs that come out when you poop. The adult worms live for a year or two. When they die you digest them and poop them out too.

Hold That Flashlight Steady

In developed countries like the United States the most common type of roundworms found in people are **pinworms.** These worms, called **Enterobius vermicularis,** are very small, about the size of a staple. Their eggs are also very small and very hardy. The eggs can live for up to two weeks on surfaces like doorknobs and telephones. If you pick up the eggs on your fingers and transfer them to your mouth they will enter your digestive system and begin to grow. Just like the ascariasis worm, this worm lives in your intestine and eats the food you eat. If that were all they did you probably wouldn't notice them. They are usually detected when the female worm lays eggs. She travels out at night to your anus to lay her eggs. If you have pinworm it's sometimes possible to see the female worm at night if you use a flashlight. The eggs are deposited on the skin around the anus. They fall off onto your bedding. Sometimes the skin itches so you scratch and transfer the eggs to your hands. Any surfaces you touch can then become covered with eggs that can be passed on to your family, friends or even strangers.

Put Your Shoes On

You might want to wear shoes if

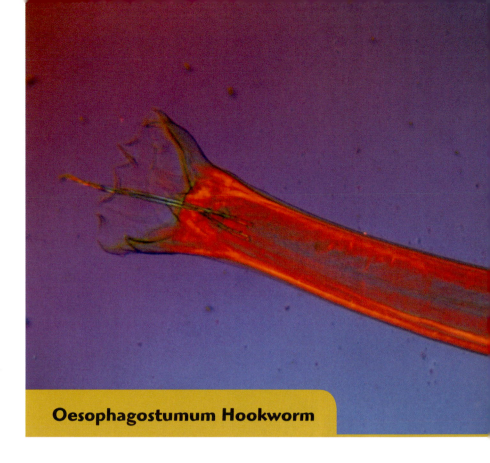

Oesophagostumum Hookworm

you live someplace hot. In warm climates, **hookworms** enter your body through the soles of your feet. These little worms live in dirt and travel between people and the soil as they grow and develop. Once they work their way in through your skin they move into your digestive system and begin to drink your blood. After a while the mature worms grow to be about ½ to ¾ of an inch in length. The female hookworm deposits eggs that move through your digestive system and leave as part of your feces.

You would think that knowing about these worms would be enough to make people avoid them. For the most part, that's true. But, some people deliberately infect themselves with hookworm. This is because hookworm infection may help reduce the symptoms of certain medical conditions such as asthma, hay fever, diabetes, Crohn's disease and multiple sclerosis. However, any benefits people get from the worm need to be carefully weighed against the possible harm due to blood loss or infection.

Measuring Tape

Imagine if you could go through life like a baby with someone else feeding you and dealing with your waste. That's the lifestyle of the **tapeworm,** a type of **flatworm.** These animals are the ultimate couch potatoes. They only eat food you've already digested so they don't even need a mouth or a digestive system. The tapeworm's knob-shaped head is called the **scolex.** The scolex has a bunch of hooks and suckers that allow the worm to attach itself to the lining of your intestine. The body of the worm looks like a long strip of tape with short detachable sections or segments called **proglottids.** Each segment contains both male and female parts of the worm and up to 100,000 eggs!

Computer image of a tapeworm

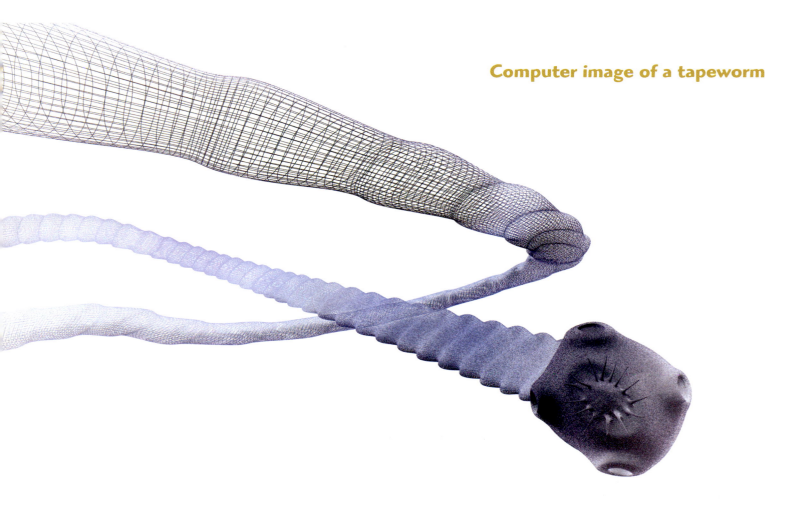

When the eggs or even a segment of the worm is released into your feces they can be eaten by the next host, which could be a pig, a cow or a fish. The eggs hatch inside this other animal and form larvae. Sometimes another animal eats the host, for example small fish are eaten by bigger fish; or the worm is released onto vegetation. Either way, the larvae eventually make their way back into something that people eat as part of a normal diet. Once eaten, the larvae attach themselves to your intestine and grow into full-sized worms at, what is for them, the all you can eat buffet.

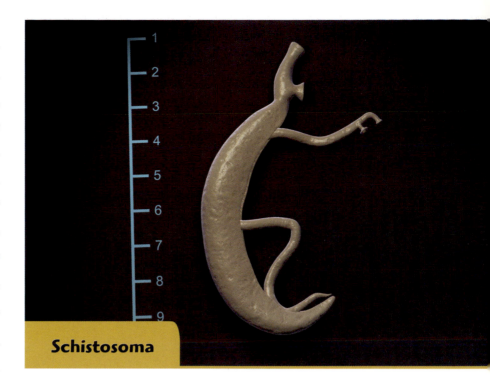

Schistosoma

It's a Fluke

Watercress salad with water chestnuts and shrimp sounds like a lovely dish for lunch, but be careful, you could become infected with a **fluke.** Flukes are a type of segmented worm, like tapeworms, which have snails as one of their hosts. We become infected when we eat freshwater plants, frogs, snails, shellfish or fish. Infection can also occur through contact with contaminated water if you drink it or bath in it. Once in your body some types of flukes like to live in your intestines, others in your liver, and some types even live in your blood. When the flukes are mature they release eggs in your feces. Efforts to reduce the number of infections have included killing or removing the snails from areas with infestations.

There's a Leech on the Beach

Leeches live in fresh water and like the other types of worms we have looked at, they are parasites.

But, the similarity stops there. Leeches don't live inside their hosts. Instead they just attach themselves to the outside. Most leeches live in freshwater, and if you go swimming where they are, they may grab onto your leg and have a drink of your blood. When they are full they will just drop off. Attachment happens with their front or rear suckers and is not painful. In fact, many people don't notice the leech is attached until they go to towel off after a swim.

For many years doctors have used leeches for medical purposes. The leech saliva contains an anaesthetic that numbs your skin. It also has a chemical called **hirudin** that stops your blood from clotting. Doctors attach medical leeches (**Hirudo medicinalis**) to areas of the skin where blood is pooling. This is done quite often after skin grafting or when amputated toes or fingers are reattached. Two or three leeches are attached and left to stay for about 40 minutes until they drop off on their own. Once the leeches have been used they must be treated as infectious waste because they contain blood from the patient.

Here Kitty Kitty

Zoonotic diseases, like ringworm (see page xx) are diseases you can get from animals, including your pets. Cats are the host of one zoonotic disease that is fairly common—**toxoplasmosis.** This disease is caused by a small single-celled creature called **Toxoplasma gondii.** This one-celled wonder, or **protozoa,** has two parts to its life cycle. The reproductive part takes place in domestic or wild cats. The growing part of the life cycle can take place in any mammal or bird, including people and cats. Once in the body the protozoa forms little sacs of fluid in the muscles and the brain.

Most people who get toxoplas-

Leech and his dinner.

Did You Know...

I Smell Nothing

People who have **anosmia** cannot detect odors. Some-one with hyposmia can't smell things as well as other people, while people with **hyperosmia** can smell things better than most people. There are people who can smell everything except for one class of things,  such as flowers, skunks or even sweat. While you wouldn't think this was much of a problem, it is. The nose acts as an early warning system and tells you if a food is rotten or if your toast is burning in the kitchen.

mosis have flu-like symptoms but otherwise don't seem to be too bothered by it. It can, however, be dangerous for the unborn babies of pregnant mothers. For this reason pregnant women are warned to have someone else clean the kitty litter box and to wear gloves when gardening.

Scientists have discovered that rats and mice infected with toxoplasmosis behave strangely. The rodents lose their fear of the smell of cat urine. Research into toxoplasmosis and human behavior has found some connection to schizophrenia and paranoia.

Amoeba's Revenge

Entamoeba histolytica is one sneaky protozoan. Not only does it kill your body's immune cells, but it also eats the cells' corpses, hiding all evidence. When it is ready to reproduce, it just splits in half...doubling its number. This creature, called an amoeba, causes a condition called **amoebic dysentery** or, as it is more commonly known, **traveler's dysentery** or **Montezuma's revenge.** You generally find out you have it when you notice that you are dashing to the bathroom with the runs (for a refresher course, see page xx). A really bad case can cause bloody diarrhea. You get amoebic dysentery by ingesting contaminated food or drinks. These foods contain human feces, either because of poor sanitation or because they have been grown with night soil—poop to most of us—used as fertilizer. Boiling water kills this amoeba, so if in doubt, boil your drinking water for at least one minute and use bottled water to brush your teeth. You can also use special pills, drops or filters to purify the water you drink.

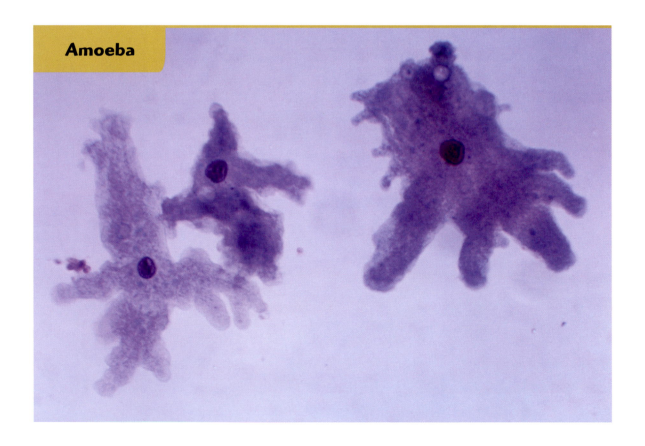

Amoeba

ANIMALS

Animals can smell gross, feel slimy and do the most disgusting things. In this section you will learn why skunks smell so bad, that Tasmanian devils really do exist and why you should always wash your hair so that it doesn't grow algae like a sloth. Be prepared to be grossed out!

Odoriferous Animals

Chemical Warfare

Most mammals have some sort of scent gland. Lift up your arm and smell your pit. That's where some of your scent glands are found.

Now, if a bear, lion or other dangerous creature were chasing you, armpit odor wouldn't help you repel the predator. What if you were a small and helpless creature? What could you do? Something as simple as strong scent glands, usually found near the anus, are the weapon of choice for many animals.

Skunks and **stink badgers** are members of the **Mephitidae** family, while polecats, minks, wolverines and weasels are members of the **Mustelidae** family. No matter what family they belong to, they stink. The source of their distinctive odor is their large anal scent glands which emit a kind of animal tear gas. These glands give off a liquid containing a bunch of stinky sulphur-containing chemicals called **thiols.** If this foul liquid hits your eyes it can cause temporary blindness. It won't kill you, but it won't make you very popular.

The Whole Zorilla

Most people have heard of skunks, but have you heard about **zoril-**

las? You won't find this animal in your backyard unless you happen to live in Africa. Zorillas are also called **striped polecats** and they are related to weasels. With white stripes down their backs, they look like skunks. However, the smell from this animal's spray makes a skunk's odor seem like finest perfume from Paris. In fact, this animal is in the running for the worst smelling creature in the world. If the smell of something can hit you from half a mile away, you just know it has to be stinky.

A liquid that comes from glands located near the animal's anus are responsible for creating this sickening smell. One whiff of this liquid and the world will spin and your eyes will burn. For such a small creature, the glands are really large.

Much like a skunk, the zorilla will give a warning before shooting. The hair on the back of the animal will stand on end and it will lift its tail. If that doesn't scare the predator away, out come the big guns and the zorilla sends off a spray of the foulest smelling liquid. The animal doesn't just spray predators, it will also

The zorilla gets its name from shortening the Spanish word for fox (zorro).

Zorilla

unleash its fury on other zorillas who are in their hood.

The Real Pepé La Pew

If you are a fan of Looney Tune cartoons, you are probably familiar with a certain charming skunk. In real life, skunks are not so loveable, especially when your pet pooch has decided to chase one. There's no hiding a skunk in your neighborhood when you're able to smell it many blocks away.

Did You Know...

Not that you'll ever try this but if your dog has been sprayed by a skunk, the spray will glow under a black light. Of course...if your pet has just been skunked, this will probably be the last thing you'll care to check out.

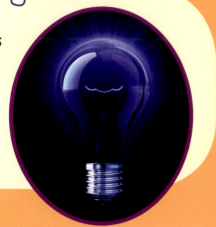

Like the zorilla, the skunk has two sets of anal glands that shoot out a distinctive liquid. When the creature goes for its daily constitutional, it will also give off some of this putrid fluid to advertise its presence to friends and enemies.

Temper Tantrum

Small children stamp their feet when they are angry. Skunks not only stamp their feet, but they lift their tails as a warning that you should back off. If a predator, dog or person doesn't take heed, the skunk will take careful aim and shoot for the eyes. And be warned: it's not just a "one shot deal" as the creature has at least six sprays in its arsenal. When

its ammo is used up, it will take a while before the skunk's body can create more.

There are certain truths in life. The chances your dog will be sprayed by a skunk are greater when:

1. It's a long weekend or a holiday and all the pet grooming places are closed.

2. You are on a hike in the woods and have to take a long car ride home with your smelly pet.

If your dog is skunked, don't believe the urban myth that tomato juice will get rid of the smell.

Musk You Smell That Way?

There are musk ox, musk deer, muskrats and even musk turtles, musk ducks and musk beetles. And there's musk from plants including musk mallow, musk root, musk clover and musk okra.

But what is **musk**? Musk refers to a strong smelling liquid that came originally from the glands of a musk deer and was traditionally used to make perfume. The word *musk* may have come from the ancient Sanskrit word for *testicles*, which gives you an idea where on the musk deer the glands containing this liquid are located.

Musk Deer

The musk deer, a now endangered species, lives in India, China, Siberia and Mongolia. The animal must be killed before the removal of the musk pod, which is the gland producing the musk. Sadly, a great many of these creatures must be slaughtered before there is enough musk to use in creating fragrances.

Once the **musk pod** is removed, the musk is collected, dried and combined with alcohol in a series of procedures. Over time the smell of the musk becomes more intense.

What does musk oil smell like? It's been described as *earthy*

Female musk ox

or like wet woods or *heavy* or just *stinky*. A little goes a long way, too, which is a good thing as it is extremely expensive. The smell of musk lasts a very long time and perfumes containing this oil will not lose their fragrance.

Civet, the Other Musk

Pity the poor civet. While this lovely animal is not killed out-right for its musk, it is kept under terrible conditions. Civets are put in small cages where they are tightly confined. People harvest the civet's musk by scraping the oil from a sac or pouch near its anal glands. This causes the animal great pain. The material is collected from both the male and female civets. The collected musk is used by the most expensive perfume manufacturers in the world. Animal rights groups have protested the use of civet musk and perfumeries are now using less of this material with a promise to stop using civet musk once the supplies they have on hand are used up. The civet oil is also a fixative or a substance that makes the perfume smell strong and last for a long time.

All That Taz

Everyone has a favorite Looney Tunes character. If yours is a certain devil who spins around the screen, then you will be delighted to learn all about the **Tasmanian Devil**.

This creature does come from an island near Australian called

Did You Know...

Good News

Scientists have been able to recreate the smell of musk in a lab so that it's not necessary to kill these deer any longer. Unfortunately, some countries still provide illegal musk oil from deer, but most companies refuse to use this material.

Tasmania, but it is not evil or possessed by the devil and it certainly does not spin around like a tornado. This is the largest meat eating marsupial in Australia and is related to koalas and kangaroos. Much like the animated animal, it has black fur with white blotches and big teeth. One feature that the cartoon never shows is that this animal stinks. As a matter of fact, the strongest skunk spray is nothing compared to this little devil. The Tasmanian Devil will shoot off its powerful spray when stressed or threatened. If you could rate its stench, you would count this spray as one of the smelliest in the world.

Are You Finished With That?

After dinner you wrap up any leftovers and put them into the fridge to eat the next day. **Wolverines,** large mammals related to the tiny weasel, have a different way of keeping other creatures away from the food they can't finish eating in one meal. These creatures are very protective of the area they live in and the food they've caught and killed. To let other wolverines know that this is their territory they use their anal scent glands to stake out their area. Much like your dog on a walk, they make sure they whizz on every available surface leaving their pee-mail for others of their species. To discourage unwanted guests from their leftovers, wolverines cover their food in pee and foul smelling liquid from their scent glands.

Spread It On Thick

Hedging Your Bets

Hedgehogs are adorable creatures that are more than just popular video game characters. In real life, these animals have a habit that makes them the perfect topic for this chapter.

For reasons scientists can't yet explain, hedgehogs perform an activity called **self anointing.** When the animal finds something with a new or unusual smell, it licks or eats the material. It then makes a spit ball in its mouth and, using its tongue, it places drops of this liquid on its spiny quills. Any creature wanting a hedgehog meal will have to first put these scent-tipped spikes in their mouths.

The smell from the paste may also hide or protect the hedge-hog from predators. Researchers think that hedgehog quills could be similar to poison tipped darts that release toxic material when they scratch predators. When they are frightened, hedgehogs curl up in a ball with these quills sticking out, acting as armor.

Not for Thanksgiving

The **turkey vulture** is not exactly the kind of bird you'd like to stuff and put on a festive table. In cartoons the bird is usually drawn as a scrawny creature with a red head and a long, hooked beak. It happily sits in a tree, waiting for something to die. This is a pretty accurate depiction.

This bird dines on dead creatures, and recent road kill makes a perfect meal. It locates its dinner by smell and is attracted to the nasty smells given off by rotting animals.

The reason these birds don't get sick from eating rotting meat is that they have a special immune system that seems to protect them from living off of things that would kill most normal animals.

The vulture also likes to smell a bit funky, too. Because the bird lives in a very hot, dry climate, it has to find a way of keeping itself cool. And it does this by peeing and pooping on its legs, a process called **urohydrosis.** If that smell weren't enough to gross out creatures who might want to dine on the vultures, the vultures have another defence. The bird vomits gross smelling, partially digested meat that can burn the eyes of any predator that gets too close.

Punk Creatures

If you don't brush your teeth it may feel like there's a slime covering your pearly whites. But how do you think a **two-toed sloth** feels? Its normally long grey or brown hair grows bluish algae. And no, not just a thin coating of algae. This stuff can grow to reach more than two feet long over several years. Now, why would any self-respecting creature allow its fur to become so icky? Well, the sloth licks the algae and draws nutrients from it. Think of the green stuff as vitamins.

Sloths are a tasty meal for larger animals like snakes and jaguars. Their best defence is to hide. So, they camouflage themselves with a greenish coat to avoid becoming dinner. In addition to being an unusual color, the sloth's thick fur protects it from the weather. It keeps off the sun and the rain.

Turkey vulture

A Revolting Diet

Tongue Straws

Try this: take a piece of toast. Cut it up into small pieces and put the pieces on a plate. Using only your tongue, try to pick up a piece of toast and put it in your mouth.

Anteaters search for food.

Now imagine doing this with a tongue that's about 2 feet long and the width of a piece of a thin ribbon with tiny spikes on the bottom. That's how an **anteater** finds dinner which is usually…..ants, and, as a special treat, termites.

Anteaters use their powerful claws to open anthills. It is a common misconception that an anteater's tongue is sticky. In fact it's the saliva of the anteater that's very sticky. As the creature puts its tongue into a mound, the ants stick to the saliva and get slurped back into the hungry anteater's mouth. The anteater doesn't just dangle its long tongue into the hole in hopes that ants will get stuck. Instead it shoots its tongue in and out of the mound about 150 times per minute!

The anteater is a large animal and can put back more than 30,000 insects a day. However, they are natural environmentalists and won't eat all the insects in the mound. Anteaters only stay at one mound for a short period of time.

I Vant To Suck Your Blood

When Bram Stoker wrote his scary book about Dracula, many people assumed he was inspired by the legend of Vlad the Impaler, a cruel ruler who lived in Romania in the 1400s. Had Stoker lived in this century he might have written about **vampire bats** instead.

There may be real vampire bats living in a cave or zoo near you. Like the fictional character, these bats like to suck the blood from unsuspecting prey. Creatures that only eat vegetables are called **herbivores,** while creatures that eat meat are called carnivores. But did you know there's a special name for creatures that like to drink blood? Vampire bats belong to this group called **sanguinivores.**

In the wild the blood of choice for this bat comes not from a blood bank but from cows or birds. These creatures don't actually bite into the blood vessels in the neck of their prey. They use their sharp teeth to break the skin of the animal, then slurp up the blood that oozes out from the cut. The attack is so swift and the bat's teeth are so sharp, the prey doesn't know it is now providing dinner for the bat. The bat's saliva has a chemi-

Fangs for the memories.

cal that keeps the blood oozing while the bat is eating. For tiny creatures, these guys can really suck back the blood. They drink almost their own body weight in blood each day.

Now for the really yucky part. After the mother bat stops nursing her offspring, she feeds her child regurgitated blood until the babies are old enough to feed on their own.

And You Thought Your Cat's Fur Balls Were Gross

Most of the things you eat eventually come out your other end. Owls have a different way of dealing with the things they eat. They rip apart, then swallow their dinners, and they aren't too fussy about things like the bones, teeth and skin. A typical meal for an owl might be a small rodent like a mouse or a bird, frog, insect or even a fluffy bunny. Inside the owl's gizzard the food is separated into two parts: things that can be broken down and things that can't be digested. And what happens to the indigestible things? Bones,

fur, teeth, feathers and other such things are formed into pellets. These pellets are then barfed up. By taking apart and studying these pellets, you can learn what an owl has been eating.

And The Winner Is...

If there were a contest for the ickiest, stickiest, smelliest and grossest creature, the award would certainly go to the **Komodo Dragon.** This "dragon" is the world's largest lizard and lives on various islands in Indonesia. Yes, one of those islands is called Komodo.

Komodo dragons stand around three feet high and can reach a whopping ten feet in length. They can weigh in at over 350 pounds, which includes the undigested food in their stomachs. These guys have huge appetites. They eat up to 80% of their body weight in one meal. Fortunately they have an expandable stomach or they might explode with that much food inside them. They are greedy, too, as very little is left over after they are finished with their kill. Whereas lions will leave about 25% of a freshly killed animal untouched, the voracious dragon will only leave about 12%. When you have chicken for supper, you don't eat the bones or the blood, you certainly don't eat the feathers and many of you might not eat the skin. The Komodo dragon eats everything: skin, bones, antlers, hooves, eyeballs, sinew and stomach…whatever body part you name, it's eaten. They even eat the intestines (first giving them a good shake to remove the feces).

If you need to eat meat as much as one of these creatures, you had better be a very effective killer. Komodo dragons bring some interesting "weapons" to the hunt. The dragons stalk their prey and can bring down large animals like water buffalo, goats and pigs. Scientists always thought that deadly bacteria in the dragon's bloody saliva infected creatures that were bitten, causing them to die. As it happens, in addition to the deadly saliva, the dragon produces a toxic venom that causes terrible pain and swelling to its prey. Even though the dragon has no sort of dental hygiene, it's not bothered by the deadly bacteria in its mouth. And, as you can

imagine, their breath is enough to knock you over--not that you're likely to want to get close enough for a whiff.

Remember the owl and how it gets rid of things it cannot digest? Now think about all the excess pieces of a goat that have gone inside a Komodo dragon. Like the owl, but on a much larger scale, the dragon upchucks the horns, skin, teeth, hooves and other indigestible material in the form of a humungous pellet covered in the smelliest mucus slime imaginable. Lest you think otherwise, these creatures aren't without **manners**. It may not be daintily done, but they wipe the mucus slime from their faces using dirt or leaves.

Komodo Dragon

Awful Amphibians

It Seemed Like a Good Idea At The Time

What relatively small creature can kill a crocodile, a poisonous snake and a large fish and can even blind a human with just a squirt of venom?

Meet the **cane toad** (**Bufo marinus**), a particularly nasty amphibian that Australia decided to import to eat the beetles living in the sugar cane fields. The toads were not effective killers of the beetles,

Giant Cane Toad

but they were really good at one thing: making more cane toads. From the initial 100 or so toads in the mid-1930s, the population of these creatures has grown to epidemic numbers. And they eat everything in sight.

You might think that the cane toad might be easy pickings for a larger creature. Strange but true, eating a cane toad, no matter what stage of life it is in, is deadly. Fish who dine on cane toad tadpoles, which in toads are more properly called **toadpoles,** die after biting these tiny tidbits. Huge venomous

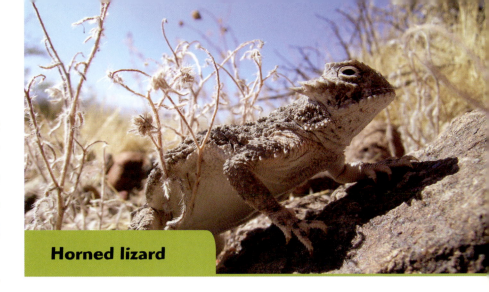

Horned lizard

snakes and crocodiles with large sharp teeth are also killed instantly when chomping down on these toads. The cane toads have no natural predators in Australia, and nothing there seems to kill them.

The cane toad has a deadly venom that comes out of its **parotoid glands** located just behind their ears. With deadly accuracy, they can shoot this venom into the mouths of unsuspecting predators. People who have been shot or sprayed with this venom in their eyes, nose or mouth suffer extreme pain. A spray in the eyes can even result in temporary blindness.

Really Blood Shot Eyes

When you are upset or sad, you cry salty tears. When the **coast horned lizard** is scared, it shoots blood from its eyes. Don't try this at home, kids. The lizard can change the blood pressure in its head. As the pressure grows, it causes tiny blood vessels in the edges of the reptile's eyes to burst. Just like a high powered water gun, the lizard then sends a spray of blood towards the predator's eyes. The spray can travel up to four feet. The shock of getting hit with blood stuns most animals, giving the lizard time to make a break for a hiding spot.

But this is not the only defence the lizard has in its bag. The creature can easily camouflage itself against its surroundings. By changing its color the lizard makes sure that predators have a hard time finding it. The lizards are quite flat or close to the ground making it difficult for birds and coyotes to pick them up. And let's not forget it's called a horned lizard. It does, indeed, have a horn that can stab the head of a predator that is trying to eat it.

And You Thought Your Backpack Was Heavy!

The next time you complain about the weight of your school books, think about the poor **Suri-**

Frog and tadpoles.

nam toad. This creature lives in cool streams in South America. The body of this toad is quite flat and it looks like a brown leaf. The female toad deposits her eggs at the surface of the water where the male fertilizes them. The eggs are then pressed into the sticky, soft-skinned back of the mother. Her back looks like a dirty sponge that has cleaned up a mass of round yellow candies. A covering forms around the eggs and, over a short period of time, the eggs begin to grow. In several months the toads are large enough to hatch from the mother's back, and they pop off like popcorn off a cob.

Sore Throat

If your voice is scratchy, people may ask if you have a **frog in your throat.** This phrase has new meaning if you were a **Darwin frog** (**Rhinoderma darwinii**).

This tiny frog from South America is the world's best amphibian dad. The female lays her eggs in wet soil and the male watches over the tadpoles for two weeks. Then, as sick as this next bit may sound, the dad gathers up the tadpole survivors and slurps them into his mouth. The babies stay in a vocal pouch in the father's mouth for about six weeks as they grow and change from tadpoles into baby frogs. Much like a cat hacking up a fur ball, the male frog throws up froglets, thereby releasing them into the world. He probably doesn't even get a Father's Day card for all his effort.

An Eye In The Back Of Their Heads

It's sometimes said that mothers have an eye in the back of their head because they can always tell what you're doing. The **tokay gecko** really does have an "eye" in the back of its head. Not an actual blinking, winking kind of eye.

Rather it is a pineal body which responds to light like an eye but doesn't form images of objects. Scientists think that the **pineal body** helps the creature deal with changing light and darkness.

If you thought that was strange, wait until you hear this. Not just content to change colors to match their background, this lizard has extra skin that folds or opens up to allow the lizard **not** to cast a shadow when hiding on a tree. In the event a predator does find the gecko and grabs it by its tail, the predator will be left holding the squirming appendage, but not the tokay. Like many lizards, this gecko can shed its tail when captured. It grows a new one over the next few weeks.

Has a doctor ever looked inside your ears with a small light? Do you think the light shines through your head and comes out the other side? Let's hope not! If a doctor were to look inside a tokay gecko's ears, or, more accurately, the small holes in the side of its head, the light would actually shine through to the other side!

Giant Leaf Frogs

Close Your Eyes And Take A Bite

Take a bite of bread. Chew and swallow. Now do this again, but this time close your eyes tightly as you swallow. Does it make any difference? Probably not. But if you were a **frog,** this is the way you would eat. Frogs don't have real teeth; they have a kind of a bumpy ridge that acts like pearly whites. These chompers aren't good for ripping or tearing food, but they are perfect for keeping the prey in place while the creature gets a strong enough hold to swallow dinner whole. This is where the eyes come in. As the frog closes its eyes tightly, the eyes sink back into its skull. This action applies pressure and actually pushes the food down the frog's throat.

Retched Reptiles

Stick 'Em Up

Put your clean bare feet up against the wall of your bedroom. Now walk up the wall to the ceiling. Unless you are part gecko, you probably didn't get very far.

Geckos have a special ability that scientists have been trying to explain for years. Using powerful microscopes, researchers have discovered the trick to the gecko's gravity-defying abilities.

Some frogs and insects have a type of glue that helps them grip a surface. Geckos don't have glue, they have dry feet. They also have tens of thousands of tiny **hairs** on their toe pads. The hairs aren't flat, but look like they've been cut at an angle. These lizards can quickly move across any surface--glass, stucco, wood--and can scurry up walls and around ceilings. But how can they stick to the wall when they only have three feet touching the surface?

It turns out they stick to walls because the unique design of their feet allows an unusual amount of the gecko's skin to touch the wall. This increases the normally tiny amounts of attractive force between the surface and the skin and makes the feet stick like glue.

Stick Out Your Tongue and Touch Your Nose

The oldest schoolyard challenge might be a dare to "stick out your

Did You Know...

tongue and touch your nose." The easiest way to win this bet is to stick out your tongue, then use your finger to touch your nose. No one said you had to touch your nose with your tongue. However, if you were a gecko, the other lizards might say, "stick out your tongue and lick your eyes."

When the gecko sticks out its tongue, it's not being rude. It's using its tongue to gather information. Gecko tongues gather particles of the smells around them and carry them back to an organ called the **Jacobson's organ** located in its mouth. This is where the gecko detects odors. Much like you, geckos have food preferences and surprise, surprise, the sweeter the food, the more the gecko will like it.

Gecko cleaning his eyes.

Close your eyes and blink. As you do this your eyelids cover your eyes. Geckos can't blink because they have no eyelids. So, to clean their eyes, they don't use eye drops, they use their tongue.

Say It. Don't Spray It

If you worked in a research laboratory and handled dangerous

Stick Out Your Tongue and Find The Cookie

Close your eyes and take a deep breath. If there are freshly baked cookies nearby, you can follow your nose to find a treat. Now stick out your tongue and see if it can help you find these sweet smelling goodies. If you were a pit viper you would be able to pinpoint the location by using your tongue and a specialized part of the roof of your mouth.

Reptiles rely on their Jacobson's Organ or vomeronasal organ to help detect information about the world around them. When the creature flicks its tongue in and out of its mouth, it's picking up chemicals in the air. Each time the animal puts its tongue back in its mouth, they touch the tongue to this organ. Signals are then sent to the snake's brain that allow it to analyze the chemicals. Using this information the snake can quickly find its prey.

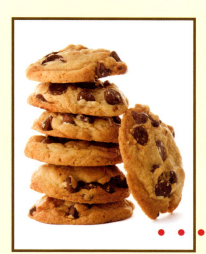

chemicals, you might expect to wear protective safely gear on your face as part of your daily routine. But why would a person working in a zoo wear these devices?

Herpetologists who work with snakes can tell you first hand why goggles or face masks are a good idea when dealing with a **red Mozambique,** a nasty kind of **spitting cobra.**

Actually these creatures don't really spit. Consider this: if you were rude enough to spit, you would save up some saliva in your mouth, suck in some air, purse your lips and blow out the gunk. This is not what the snakes are doing.

A spitting cobra tightens its muscles and squeezes the glands that contain the deadly venom. This pressure pushes the venom through a hole in its long fangs. As the venom is forced through the fangs, the cobra takes a deep breath and blows. This creates a spray, much like an aerosol pump that delivers window cleaner. Except, the snake's spray travels up to ten feet!

Snakes that kill their prey by squeezing them to death have

Mozambique Spitting Cobra

fangs that face inwards or towards their throats. This is so that when they bite down on their prey, the prey cannot pull away from the snake. In cobras, the fangs face out of their mouths towards their prey and, more importantly, their prey's eyes.

If the venom lands on your skin, it does no harm. However, put that stuff in your eyes, it burns. The toxins can do so much damage to the sensitive tissues in your eyes you may even go blind.

Sonoran Coral Snake

Stand Back!
It's Going to Blow

When some snakes are frightened or wish to frighten you, they rattle or hiss. Others, like cobras, may rear up, flare their large facial hoods, and spit venom in your direction. Boas may sink their long teeth into you and then wrap themselves around you so you cannot breath. So be afraid. Be very afraid…when you run into the **Sonoran Coral Snake.** This reptile's main source of defence is farting in your general direction. There is even a scientific term for this, **cloacal popping.** The farts don't last long but are loud enough to be heard several feet away. And it's not just one fart but a whole symphony of toots. No one has ever taken an air quality sample, so there's no report describing the smell of these farts.

The farts don't appear to be related to a diet of beans or other foods that cause gas build up. The Sonoran Coral Snake creates a fart in much the same way as a human would: it forces air out its sphincter. It's not as disciplined as people and occasionally other things shoot out of the anus. It also draws air back into the anus and can continue this *terrifying* noise for a long period of time. The response to these farts from any nearby predatory animal might well be uncontrollable laughter, in which case the snake has time to make its escape.

THINGS IN THE OCEAN

Before you go for a dip in the sea, you might want to acquaint yourself with some of the creatures beneath your feet or swimming next to you. Perhaps you might want to check the shellfish you eat before you pop it in your mouth. Is there anything hiding in there?

Just When You Thought It Was Safe To Go Into The Water

Cucumber Shoes

Despite their descriptive name, **sea cucumbers** are not vegetables you put in a seafood salad. This really strange creature is an **echinoderm** and it's related to starfish, sea urchins and sand dollars.

It looks and feels like a soft, rotting vegetable cucumber with spikes. Some sea cucumbers have a unique way of protecting themselves against predators. Rather than running away or fighting back, they poop out their innards through an opening called the cloaca in the rear end of their body. There's even a name for this process: evisceration. Not to worry, the creature will grow replacement parts in a short period of time.

If that isn't weird enough, the natives of the island of Palau in the western Pacific Ocean have chosen to wear this creature's guts as footwear instead of brand name sneakers. The people grab any sea cucumber that's handy and, in the same way you squeeze toothpaste from a tube, they squish out the innards from a sea cuke over their bare feet. The sticky goop expelled by the animal protects their feet from the sharp reefs. The obliging sea cucumber is then placed back into the ocean to live another day.

Projectile Vomit

Have you ever been so sick that you've "thrown up your guts?" While it may feel like that, your stomach is still safely inside your body. That expression, however, has real meaning when you are a **thornback ray (Raja clavata)**.

This creature gobbles its food whole. It doesn't take small bites and chew before swallowing like your mother tells you to do. Which means that the thornback ray sucks up skin, bones, cartilage, eyeballs and anything else that makes up their dinner.

Once inside the ray's stomach, the food begins to breakdown and the ray absorbs the nutrients.

If you think that the materials that can't be digested are pooped out, think again. The ray hurls its garbage. And it doesn't just vomit out the leftovers. It throws up its entire stomach! Once its stomach is outside its body, the thornback gives its head a good shake to clean off the debris. Then, using strong muscles in its gut and throat, it pulls its stomach back in through its mouth.

All of this doesn't take very long, only a few seconds. Scientists who have conducted tests on the rays have learned that they can make the ray upchuck by giving it small doses of poison. The poison isn't enough to hurt the creature, it just makes it feel yucky enough to barf.

Thornback Ray *(Raja clavata).*

In Deep Water No One Can Hear You Scream!

While you might be a little young for this, your parents or grandparents may remember a movie from the 1970s featuring a truly scary creature. The monster in the movie *Alien* had a series of jaws that shot out of its mouth. Talk about an overbite! This was enough to give most adults nightmares. But little did the special effects people ever think that something like this could live on earth.

Enter the **moray eel.** Obviously this is not a newly discovered creature, but one feature of this animal was recently observed for the first time. Like the fictional monster in *Alien*, the moray eel has a second set of jaws located inside its throat. These are called **pharyngeal jaws** and they are unique to this eel.

The eel uses its first set of teeth to chomp down on its prey as it swims past. The eel's strong jaws and sharp teeth hold the prey in place as the second set of jaws come up from its throat. And, just like the creature in the movie, these jaws take hold of the poor fish and pull it down into the eel's esophagus.

Scientists have studied other creatures with these kinds of jaws but never one that had teeth.

Mosaic moray eel

The Slimy Green Machine

What do you think would be the least expensive way to light a

Christmas tree? Yes, you could purchase energy-efficient bulbs, or you could limit the amount of time the lights were turned on, or you could find yourself an **electric eel.** This is exactly what someone did in Japan in 2007.

Harnessing the power from an eel is not that difficult. A large electric eel is placed in a tank that has been fitted with two aluminum panels. As the eel sends off an electric charge, the panels collect the charge and pass it to wires connected to the panels. The charge is large enough to provide the power to turn on the lights of a Christmas tree. The eel isn't always "on" and so the lights go on and off depending on the discharge from the fish.

In the wild, eels use their power to stun their prey or scare off predators that want to eat them. The eel can give off about 500 volts and 1 ampere of current. This is enough zap to harm or even kill a person. The electricity is made inside the eel chemically in much the same way as a battery or dry cell makes electricity. Most animals make some electricity, the eel is unusual in

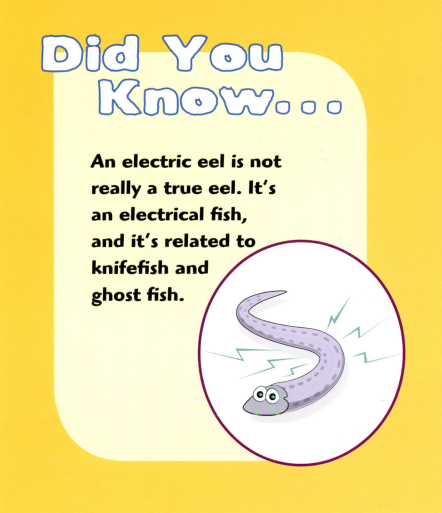

Did You Know...

An electric eel is not really a true eel. It's an electrical fish, and it's related to knifefish and ghost fish.

that it makes a lot of energy and it releases it externally.

Ice Running Through Your Veins

Warm blood pumps through your body, and anti-freeze runs through your car. Both liquids keep things going in cold weather. There are a number of creatures who have things backwards: they have a kind of anti-freeze keeping them alive in icy conditions.

The **Antarctic icefish** lives in a very hostile environment. It couldn't get much colder. Scientists have discovered that this fish has an antifreeze **glycoprotein** in their blood as well as in other bodily fluids. This keeps the fish from turning into an icicle in the freezing water.

On the other hand, some animals allow themselves to freeze solid. The **Canadian wood frog** spends the winter as solid as a skating rink. Nearly every part of this creature freezes and the majority of the frog's body turns to ice. If you lifted the frog's eyelids you would find that they have turned white because they are frozen. Normally if ice forms in a living creature, it will kill the animal. Scientists have been studying these frogs to find out how their bodies can freeze, thaw and even freeze again. They are amazed that the frog can be revived from a state of suspended animation.

I Don't Do Windows

The **cleaner fish** (**Labroides dimidiatus**) is basically the car wash of the ocean. This tiny creature takes on the task of cleaning larger fish of parasites that are growing on the host. Fish don't have hands, so they cannot take a cloth and

Did You Know...

When some people die, they pay to have their bodies frozen in special facilities. They hope to be thawed out when medical technology can bring them back to life and cure them of the disease that killed them.

wipe themselves off when things get on their skin. This is where the cleaner fish comes in handy.

It Pays to Advertise

The tiny fish approaches the larger fish and does a "dance." If the fish wishes to be vacuumed, it will exhibit certain behaviors such as opening its mouth, staying still or showing its side to the cleaner.

The cleaner now knows it has been invited to touch the larger fish and will proceed to eat all the parasites growing on the host. The cleaner is very thorough, going under the gills, down the body and even into the mouth of the other fish.

The entire process is not unlike going to the dentist to have your teeth cleaned. A dentist uses sharp tools to scrape guck off your teeth. Inside the mouth of the cleaner fish are four large canine-like teeth that help pry the attached parasites from the body.

The fish even set up **cleaning stations** where divers have observed that fish line up waiting to be scrubbed. Host fish can even

A Wrasse cleaning a Coral Grouper

recognize a cleaner fish who has serviced them before. The relationship between the animals is called **cleaning symbiosis.** In this type of relationship one fish gets cleaned at the same time the other fish gets food. It's a pretty good deal for both.

Scary Scales

Defensive Armor

Some creatures have sharp quills or spines to protect them from predators. Others have poisons to prevent them from being eaten.

Some use hard casings or shells to stop attacks. But what about a protective layer of slime?

Fish are slimy. There's no other way of looking at this goop which covers all parts of the creature from the tip of its nose down the scales and even onto its skin.

Freshwater fish (below) and Perch (above)

What exactly is this yucky stuff? While humans don't appreciate this material, fish couldn't live without it. The slime is a kind of **mucoprotein** that is manufactured by the creature. It protects the animal against things that can make it sick like parasites, bacteria and fungus.

The skin of a fish is quite fragile and any rips or tears can harm the creature. Even if you catch a fish in a net and release it, you may still hurt it as the fish will

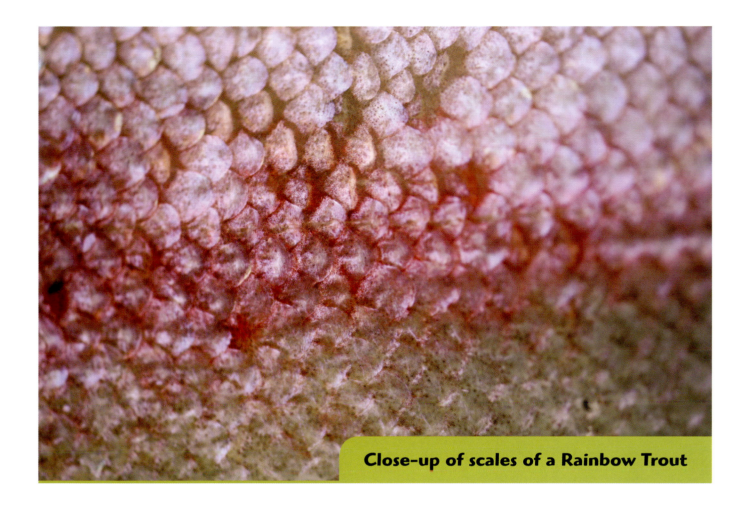

Close-up of scales of a Rainbow Trout

bleed **electrolytes** (fluids containing salts and minerals) when it is placed back into the wild. When the slime coating is rubbed off or touched, the fish is more likely to get an infection or die.

The slime may look and feel yucky, but the coating has special antibodies and enzymes or chemicals. Just like sunscreen that protects people from the harmful rays of the sun, the slime helps keep the fish's scales and skin healthy.

Tongue Tied

Try this: stick out your tongue and try to roll it into a tube. Some of you can do this. Some of you cannot. Researchers still can't agree on exactly how you get this ability, but one thing is certain, the **archer fish** inherited this trait from its parents.

These fish have an interesting way of catching dinner: they shoot it out of the air. No, they

Speaking of scales, there are different kinds found on fish. You can even tell how old a fish is by counting the rings found on the cycloid or ctenoid scales. The more rings, the older the fish.

don't use a bow and arrow. Archer fish roll their tongues into a tube and push water through this tube. When the high powered spray of water hits an unsuspecting bug, it causes the bug to fall into the water where the fish quickly gobbles up its prize.

Sometimes several archer fish will hunt together, each shooting spit at an insect. As the prey falls, the fish may not wait until it hits the water. Instead it will jump out to grab the insect before another fish can eat it.

Archer fish jumping for insect

CREEPY CRAWLERS

I want to suck your blood. No, it's not a vampire. It's the spider beside her. Check out the strange habits of the creepy crawly things on a branch near you.

Stinky Bugs

Green stink bug

The Name Says It All

Pity the poor **stink bug.** Not only is it saddled with a pretty nasty name, but it also lives up to it. These creatures don't smell because they sweat or because they don't take baths.

Shield bugs and stink bugs have a gland in their thorax, located between their first and second pair of legs, which creates a yucky liquid. Creatures that want to eat the insect are too grossed out by the smell to bite down on the tender morsel.

If you are really interested, the main chemical in the liquid is called **trans–2–hexenal** and it acts both to protect the bug and to signal and attract its mate.

There are so many stinky things in the world, how do you know you've met one of these bugs?

Their odor has been described as being musky, bitter and sharp with hints of sour apple, banana and almond. Fortunately, if they get into your house they won't harm anything, and they don't carry any human diseases. Don't pick them up though. They've been known to prick people with their mouth parts.

Don't Call Me A "Potty Name"

Dung beetles have the worst name, but they have earned it because they eat.....you guessed it, dung. Their food of choice can come from the feces of just about any creature. They favor all poop; it doesn't matter if the food has been fully digested or partially digested. These bugs don't even need to drink water as they get everything they need to survive from their revolting food source.

Dung beetles have specially shaped heads that acts as excavation tools to help them dig up and roll dung into balls. These balls of poop can be taken back to their homes or buried in the ground to be eaten at a later date. How's this for romance? A male dung beetle rolls a giant ball of manure and gives it to a female as a gift so that she will accept him as a mate. Much like a man giving a woman a diamond, the bigger the better! Females lay eggs in the balls of fresh dung and the dung protects and acts as food for the larvae inside. Adults prefer to sip on the tasty liquid squeezed from these balls of feces.

These beetles are great for the environment. They eat or bury waste, which makes the ground rich in nutrients and keeps the area from being overrun with feces from wild animals. Dung beetles are nature's pooper scoopers and help to reduce the numbers

Did You Know...

You Look Like A God To Me

The ancient Egyptians used to worship the scarab, which is a classy name for the dung beetle or images made of the dung beetle. These images were often made from stone and precious materials.

Centipedes and millipedes aren't insects. They're related to shrimp, lobsters and crabs.

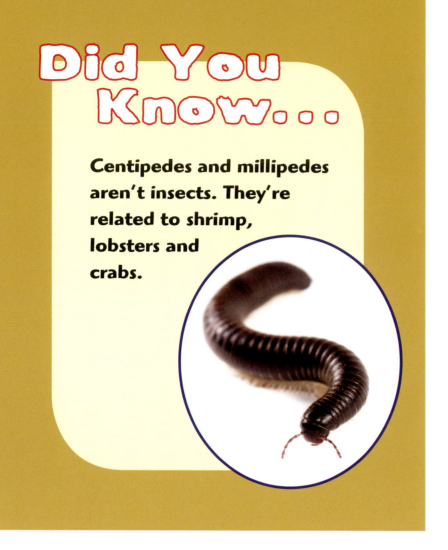

and long legs that stick out from their bodies and their bite can hurt as much as a bee's sting. Millipedes are round and kind of cute. They have tiny legs that make the creature move in a wave motion, and they don't bite at all.

But let's get to the interesting and smelly part. Millipedes have a smell that contains toxic chemicals that harm critters that want to eat them. They give off a gas called **hydrogen cyanide,** a highly poisonous chemical. This gas can ooze out from each and every segment of the millipede's body. Given the size of the creature, this is quite a feat (or feet, as the case might be). Other predator-repellent chemicals millipedes have in their arsenal include **benzoquinones and alkaloids.**

of flies and other pests who also dine on the droppings.

My Milli-Peed On Me!

How can you tell if the creature that just scurried across your floor is a **millipede** or a **centipede**? No, you don't have to count its legs. Even if you did, centipedes don't have 100 legs as their name suggests and millipedes certainly don't have a thousand.

Centipedes have flat bodies

While a centipede's bite can really hurt people, the tiny amounts of hydrogen cyanide in a millipede's scent smells quite pleasant to our senses. It's been described as being similar to almond extract or paste. This is not to say you need to prove this by handling a millipede.

Walk That Walk

Come Into My Parlor

The next time you are out on a walk, take a close look at a spider's web, preferably one with a spider on it. Find a stick and gently touch one of the threads, but be careful not to break the web.

Does the spider move towards the stick to see if dinner is caught in the sticky web? Even if it doesn't move in the direction of the stick, it will probably quickly and nimbly scurry across the web. This raises the logical question: why don't spiders stick to their own webs and what makes the webs sticky?

Spiders have special **spinneret gland**s in their abdomens that create the silk-like threads. The spinnerets are designed to do specific jobs. When the arachnid weaves its web it makes both sticky and non-sticky threads. They don't stick to their own web because they become expert at traveling on the non-sticky threads and because they have an oily substance that oozes from their feet to keep them from sticking.

If you use a magnifying glass you will see that some of the threads look like they have drops of liquid strung along a thin line. Other threads are smooth. Spiders also create a special line that acts like a dinner bell. When something becomes stuck in the web, the tug on this line alerts the creature that food as arrived.

Wolf spider

Precision Marching

It would be fun to be able to walk up the sides of walls and dance across the ceiling like a fly, ant or bee. Not only can these small insects perform this astonishing feat, but they can do this while carrying food that weighs even more than they do. Using powerful microscopes scientists have found that the bottoms of insects' feet are covered with a sticky substance. When an insect steps on a surface these adhesive pads automatically come out from the base of the creature's foot. This allows the insects to appear to defy gravity and walk upside down. The pads are very sensitive and allow the insect to tell if a surface is rough like wood or smooth like glass. If they need a strong grip the "claws" can extend further to assist the insect's movement. It turns out that the insects employ a kind of hydraulic system to move these claws. Fluid moves through compartments in the insect's leg and makes the claws extend and retract.

Can't Touch This

Assassin bug

Ninja Bugs

The **assassin bug,** much like its name, is a quick and effective killer. They use the sticky food pads on the bottom of their feet to hold their dinner in place.

The assassin bug doesn't use a gun or knife to slay its prey. Instead it turns its dinner into a liquid meal.

The assassin bug has a sharp, pointed beak or **rostrum** that stabs the victim's body. Then a squirt a poison into the body causes the muscles and nerves to turn to jelly. Basically the insides of the prey's body turns into a drinkable mush. The assassin bug then uses its beak like a straw to suck up its meal.

This killer bug is not afraid to take on prey much larger than itself. Its toxins are so deadly that it can kill critters in only a few seconds. Dinner can last several weeks if the assassin bug bagged something huge like a cockroach or caterpillar.

Handle with care! Some assassin bugs do not like to be handled and can shoot this poison towards the face of its attacker. If you are hit in the eyes with this liquid it can be painful and even cause temporary blindness.

Mind Control

When I Say "Jump," You Say "How High?"

Grasshoppers and **crickets** like to hop around, but one place they don't dive into is water. There are times, however, when these normally non-swimming insects jump into a situation that is certain death. Why?

The **nematomorph hairworm** (**Spinochordodes tellinii**) is a parasite that hatches inside these insects. It grows and grows until it is time for the worm to return to the water and become an adult.

Scientists are studying how this invader can take over the mind of the grasshopper forcing it to do an activity that goes against its very nature. Most creatures want to live and don't take chances with their lives. The parasite only affects certain behaviors. For example, it doesn't stop the insect from eating or sleeping. At the appropriate time, these worms produce a chemical that goes to the grasshopper's brain and takes control of the insect's actions, forcing it to take that big watery leap. Once the insect has landed in the water, the parasite pops out, much like a creature from a scary movie, and the host grasshopper dies. The hairworm proceeds to find a mate and the cycle begins again.

Broadcast Antennas

Snails don't normally like to broadcast their location to birds that might try to eat them, but when they have a hitchhiker aboard they do just that. A snail **parasite** called **Leucochloridium paradoxum,** a flatworm, tricks the snail into thinking it's safe in the dark even when it's out in bright light. The cycle begins when snails eat the parasite's eggs that have been deposited on leaves as part of bird droppings. The eggs hatch and the tiny worms grow. The worms move into the snail's tentacles, causing the tentacles to swell and change color. These tentacles now look like a worm or caterpillar, the favorite foods of many birds. When the snails move into the light, these beaconing tentacles attract birds. A bird takes a bite of the tentacle and the worms are swallowed. Fortunately this doesn't usually kill the snail. The worms reproduce in the birds and their eggs are released in bird poop to begin the adventure once more.

You Smell Familiar

The alcon blue butterfly (maculinea) has found a way to create a private day care for their caterpillar "babies." The beautiful butterfly coats its larvae in a chemical that smells like ant's larvae. The butterflies then leave their larvae on plants. The larvae hatch into caterpillars that are then found by ants who caretake the caterpillars. If you smell like an ant, you must therefore be an ant. This is called **chemical mimicry.**

Garden snail and dinner

The Blob

Attack Of The Slime Mold

Perhaps you've heard of a social butterfly, but have you ever heard of a social amoeba? We kid you not.

There is something called a **slime mold** and it is one of the strangest things you will find on a walk in the wild.

The next time you come across something on the ground in a wooded area that looks like yellow animal vomit, take a closer look. You may be in the presence of Dictyostelium discoideum.

Scientists study this mold because it doesn't behave like anything they've ever seen. These molds start out like normal fungus with separate single cells, much like yeast, but when their food supply becomes limited, thousands of these cells clump together to form a large colony that acts like a single creature.

When you grow a fungus like yeast in a bowl, it doesn't climb out and search for food. But these molds don't just stay on the ground and grow there. This super slime goes hunting for food. Moving at the blinding speed of one centimeter per hour (okay, it's really very slow), it rampages through the forest looking for food. Don't worry. It won't attack you or your pet. It prefers

Slime mold looks like animal vomit

to consume bacteria, decomposing leaves and organic material. When food runs low, it stops and releases spores that travel on the wind to grow in another place.

But That's Not All!

Slime molds don't just move around randomly. Scientists in Japan found that the slime mold **Physarum polycephalum** could make its way through a plastic maze to find food. The mold doesn't just grow to fill up the maze, instead it moves through the maze in

the most efficient way possible, avoiding all the dead ends.

Scientists aren't exactly sure how the mold does this, but they describe the mold as "clever and cunning."

We're Here for a Good Slime

Healthy corals are slimy. They seem to be covered in a layer of snot. Until recently scientists believed that the only reason slime covered corals was to protect coral communities from drying out at low tide. They were so wrong. Corals create this gooey topping for an even more important purpose: they provide a home to bacteria and fungi that keep the creatures healthy.

Zooxanthellae, a single celled algae living in corals, is responsible for giving corals their bright colors and for creating nutrients that feed the creatures. In turn, corals create slime using these enriched materials. This mucus is made of sugars, carbohydrates and other yummy materials. It's so sticky that other nutrients floating by will attach to the slime.

You might think that something covered in slime would die because it couldn't eat or breathe. These algae make their own air and use the water and gases dissolved in the water to make food for themselves and the coral. This slime not only keeps the creatures fed but healthy. It's the equivalent of eating chicken soup when you have a cold. The slime makes its own form of antibiotic or penicillin of the sea.

Coral exposed at low tide

PLANTS

Smell the roses, but be careful smelling some of these babies. Be happy that you eat plants and that plants cannot eat you...or can they? Welcome to the world of carnivorous greenery and putrid flowers.

Greens that Eat You

Feed Me Seymour

In the musical *Little Shop of Horrors* a hungry plant named Audrey II needs people in the worst way—as dinner! The good news is that giant people-eating plants from outer space don't really exist, but huge plants that eat insects do.

Look around. One may even be in a garden close to you. Welcome to the gross world of **carnivorous plants** that dine on insects.

Like people, plants need food, water and light. Plants that get more of these things tend to grow bigger and stronger than plants living in more hostile conditions. Lucky plants that grow in homes and gardens will be fertilized and watered so they don't have to develop ways of finding the essentials.

Plants in the wild have to live off the nutrients they find in the soil. Needed water can come from the ground, lakes or streams or from precipitation like rain or dew. But what happens when the place a plant grows isn't very rich in nutrients or the soil is thin, acidic or rocky? What's a plant to do? Turns out some of them become carnivores.

While there are many different species of carnivorous or insectivorous plants, there are only a few basic ways that plants capture their prey.

Hey Pitcher, Pitcher

Pitcher plants are great examples of pitfall traps which is one of the ways plants capture insects. As the name suggests, these plants look like long, leafy pitchers or vases. The size and shape of the pitcher varies, depending on the kind of plant. Some plants have long, thin cups while others have fatter, deeper cups. They live in areas where the soil is acidic or not rich in nutrients.

Looks Aren't Everything

Pitcher plants look attractive to the average flying or crawling insect because they have bright colors and sweet nectar. A greedy bug lands on the plant, then keeps going deeper and deeper into the plant only to discover that it can't get out. Even if it turns around, it encounters sharp downward facing spines that prevent the bug from escaping. The creature eventually drowns when it finds itself in the bottom of the pitcher in a pool of liquid called **phytotelmata.** Slowly the bug's body starts to dissolve, eaten away by either bacteria or enzymes created by the plant. Some plants allow insect larvae to live in their pitcher or bulb. For that extra little treat, the plant is more than happy to digest the poop from the larvae.

Much like food in your stomach, the plant breaks down the insects and creates the mineral nutrients it needs to survive. Do these plants like the taste of bugs? It's not a question of eating an insect that makes the plant

Pitcher plant

salivate. It's simply a matter of plant survival. When prey is dissolved, necessary flora **vitamins** such as phosphorus and nitrogen are released.

I'm A Mazed

Some pitcher plants have maze-like chambers. At the mercy of a bewildering number of false exits, the confused prey wanders further into the trap to oblivion.

Sticks To You Like Flypaper

Unlike fancy electric zappers, flypaper is an old-school way of getting rid of pesky insects. A very sticky and sometimes poisonous strip is hung near a kitchen or outdoor eating area. As **airborne** insects land on the surface of the paper, they find themselves stuck there for good. Much like this store-bought invention, a **flypaper trap plant** captures its meal when an insect lands on its glue-like leaves. The **butterwort** plant is a great example of this variety of carnivorous greenery. As the name suggests it has a buttery

or greasy surface. What insect can resist the shiny and sweet smelling leaves? The leaves have two glands: one that creates the creamy liquid and a second that produces digestive fluids. When a trapped insect discovers it cannot move its feet or wings, it does the natural thing—it tries to escape. The more it struggles, the more it becomes attached. This movement signals the plant that dinner has arrived, and the leaves begin to close around the prey. Once the bug is fully enclosed by the plant, it's digested and used for nutrients.

The **sundew** is another flypaper trap plant that you may have seen. These beautiful plants have red tips that glisten with what looks like dew or nectar, which

Butterwort

Sundew

trap. You can find these in plant stores and some science toy stores. This plant looks like a green clam with spiky frills along the edge. It has tiny sensory hairs on the inside surface of each leaf. This plant is part of the snap trap species of insect-eating plants. If you look closely at the leaves you can see they are slightly convex or bent outwards. When something touches the sensitive hairs, the two sides snap inwards and become concave. This action is so quick that the prey doesn't have time to escape.

is exactly what flies think they're seeing. These shiny tips have glands that make enzymes that eat the poor insect stuck to them.

Birth of Venus

The carnivorous plant that most people recognize is the **Venus fly-**

It's easy to see how this plant captures its dinner. It's harder to explain how the leaves move so quickly. A complicated series

Venus Fly Trap

of steps involving electrical impulses and transfer of chemicals causes plant cells at the base of the trap to swell up with water and close the trap. This process uses up lots of the plant's energy, so don't tease a Venus flytrap by making it close on nothing or you can kill the plant. The process where plants move in response to touch is called **thigmotropism.**

Flea Collar

Right about now you're asking yourself, "Are there any carnivorous plants in the water?" Why, yes there are. The **Aldrovandaare** is related to the Venus flytrap but grows in water and not on land. It's a snap trap plant whose traps are found in spirals located around a central stem. This explains why it is commonly called the **water wheel plant.** Most insects don't live under water, and this plant's diet consists of tiny crustaceans including **water fleas** (**daphnia**). These plants are extinct in most of the world. Today, they are found mainly in Australia and Poland.

Did You Know...

Fool Me Once

Since the Venus flytrap doesn't have eyes, how can it tell the difference between an insect and something without any food value? Why waste time and energy closing if there's no payoff? The plant has developed an interesting way of deciding when to close. If several of the sensory hairs have been triggered at a certain interval, it presumes that food has arrived and snaps shut. So the plant responds to the motion of the object and not its food value.

It's Not Easy Being Green

Corpse Flower

William Shakespeare once wrote that "a rose by any other name would smell as sweet." While this is true, it seems probable that a posy called the **corpse flower** would probably smell like a rotting, dead body.

The real name for this large bouquet is the **titan arum** or **Amorphophallus titanum,** which roughly translated from Ancient Greek means "giant funny looking penis." It also goes by an Indonesian name, **Bunga bangkai** or corpse or cadaver flower.

The world's worst smelling and largest flower grows wild only in Sumatra. You'll also find them cultivated in botanical gardens around the world. This is not the kind of plant you can put on your kitchen table. It's so large it requires a room and ventilation all its own. The flower can reach over nine feet in height!

The plant looks like something from a science fiction horror movie. It has a huge, single, dark purple leaf or **spathe** wrapped around a tall cone or **spadix** that sticks out from the center of its structure. The spadix heats up to about a human's body temperature and this causes its fetid smell to travel a great distance.

Titan Arum in bloom.

The putrid smell and purple color deceive insects into thinking they're seeing and smelling rotting flesh. Rotting flesh is the dinner bell for flesh flies and carrion eating beetles, which are more than happy to pollinate the flower when it blooms. Of course, that only happens every four to ten years. Both the male and the female flowers of the plants are in the spadix. The female flower blooms first, and the male flower opens a day or so later. This prevents the plant from self-fertilizing.

FOOD

You would think that this would be a safe section. Nothing can harm you here. But cheese can wiggle. Vomit is in your tea. Coffee beans are full of feces and fish can kill you. Be afraid. Be very afraid.

Are You Sure That's Edible?

Who Cut The Cheese?

If the only cheese you're familiar with is the kind that comes wrapped in plastic and smells like its wrapper, then you're in for a treat. Welcome to the world of really smelly food. One of the smelliest is **cheese.**

Let's begin with how cheese is created. Cheese begins with milk from cows, goats or any other mammal that gives milk. Throw in some bacteria, molds and other microorganisms, add some heat and, as the French would say, voilà, you have the making of a sandwich. Of course it can take time and special conditions to produce the best cheese. Cheese can be hard and cured or soft and runny. Some come with rinds, others with wax, while some are even covered with straw, ash or a material that rivals the bottom of the kitty litter box.

The stinkiest cheeses may contain bacteria called **Brevibacterium linens.** This little bug gives cheese a nice orangey-pink outside layer and fills it with flavorful chemicals. Some cheeses have the aroma of dirt, mushrooms, rotten eggs or stinky feet. The truly stinky ones are an acquired taste, so don't knock them 'til you've tried them.

Did We Mention The Rennet?

One of the tradition components of cheese making is **rennet.** This is the gross part: rennet is a mixture of proteins made from the lining of a calf's stomach and it causes milk to coagulate or gather together. A similar material can also be produced by bacteria or even in a lab which means vegetarians can enjoy this food.

Don't Bring This To School For Lunch

The smell of some fruits like limes, lemons, oranges, apples, and strawberries is so wonderful that manufacturers use these fragrances in all kinds of popular products like dishwashing detergents, hand lotions, soaps and even air fresheners. But the one fruit whose smell will never be used is the **durian.**

This fruit from Southeast Asia is about the size of a football and is covered with sharp prickles. When you cut it open it has white, yellow or orange pulp with an interesting taste. But, many people never get to the taste because the smell gets to them first.

The best way to describe the odor of ripe durian is hot horse manure with fried onions and garlic served in a sewage tank and covered in vomit. Okay, maybe that's a bit harsh. There is some variability in the odor, and many people enjoy eating this fruit. Animals in the wild can smell the ripening fruit from at least half a mile or more away. These creatures aren't nearly as grossed out by the odor as humans and are more than happy to make a meal of the fruit. The seeds of the fruit do what most seeds do and

Durian fruit.

pass through the animal. When pooped out the seeds land in natural fertilizer pots and sprout.

Chemists have studied the durian to find out what makes it smell so bad. They found the worst offender in the durian aroma may be hydrogen sulphide gas, the same thing that makes rotten eggs smell. Other chemicals were found including other sulphur compounds.

Iron sulphide in hard boiled egg.

Wake Up and Smell the Sulphur

What do rotten eggs, stink bombs and volcanoes have in common? They all smell like sulphur. It's easy to see why stink bombs and volcanoes have that smell; they both contain this chemical.

But what about eggs? How does something that comes from inside a chicken contain this smelly substance?

Have your parent hard boil an egg, then peel it and cut it in half. Can you see a line of color between the yolk and the white? The bluish grey ring is made of a chemical called **iron (II) sulphide.** Cooking releases iron from the yolk of the egg and the iron combines with sulphur released from the proteins in the egg white. The sulphur in egg whites can also come out as hydrogen sulphide gas, which gives boiled eggs a slight odor.

The hydrogen sulphide in rotten eggs is much stronger smelling because there's more of it. Bacteria break down the egg proteins even more than cooking the egg.

You Ate WHAT?

I Like Vomit In My Tea

Would you ever eat barf? Would you ever eat the barf of an insect? Yuck! How about this? Do you like honey on your toast? If your answer is "yes," then you do like eating vomit…insect vomit.

Perhaps you've never thought much about where your food comes from. In the case of honey, it's made by **honeybees.** These bees use their tongues to collect sweet nectar from flowers and store it in a sac on their bodies. Back at the hive, they pass along this nectar to the mouths of other bees. These bees chew the liquid and add an enzyme. This process will cause the water to evaporate from the nectar. Then bees **regurgitate** (the polite word for **puke**) this sweet goop into individual honeycomb cells. When the honey is thick and sticky, the honeycomb is sealed with wax. Bees don't make honey for people. They make it as food for the hive.

Really Fast Food

In some places the phrase, "Waiter, there's a fly in my soup!" takes on a whole new meaning. People in the United States aren't delighted to discover an insect in their meal, but in other places around the

According to a recent study, giving children with sore throats a teaspoon of buckwheat honey works better to sooth their throats than over the counter cough medicine.

world, edible insects can be the main course. As disgusting as it may sound to you, insects are an excellent and inexpensive source of protein. And they have little fat. Unlike animals such as cows and chickens that consume a tremendous amount of resources in water, land and food, insects are plentiful and easy to obtain. Bugs also contain high levels of the vitamins and minerals that people need in their diets. Consider this: a cricket contains less than half the calories and only one quarter of the fat of the same amount of ground beef. And it naturally contains calcium, phosphorous, iron, thiamine, riboflavin and niacin.

What kind of bugs might you eat? In Africa you might find kungu cakes which contain small flies called midges. In Thailand, you will find crickets, locusts, mealworms and water bugs. And let's not forget chocolate-covered insects found in many gourmet stores. Be careful though, some insects are poisonous. You don't want to pop one in your mouth without checking first.

Where's That Coffee Been?

In some places in the United States and Canada, it's difficult not to find a certain coffee company on almost every corner. But there's one blend you won't find in your local café. It's called **kopi luwak** and one cup can cost you as much as $50.

Civets, wild cat-like creatures,

pluck ripe red coffee cherries off trees. Picture an animal that looks like a cross between a racoon and a spotted house cat, add in bulgy eyes and you get the picture. They are picky eaters and choose only the sweetest berries, first nibbling off the outer coating. Then they swallow the rest and in the stomach, as usual, things begin to break down. In particular, this process removes some of the caffeine and changes the taste of the coffee bean. Like most things that aren't digested, the beans are eventually pooped out.

This is where humans come in. People poke through civet poop searching for the "recycled" coffee beans. The bean is cleaned, processed, roasted, packaged and sold for as much as $600 per pound. Because the bean is so rare and so difficult to find, people are willing to pay silly prices for the bragging rights of owning this pooped coffee.

Saliva Soup

Which would you rather have: a top of the line video game system with a flat screen TV and

Civet resting on a branch.

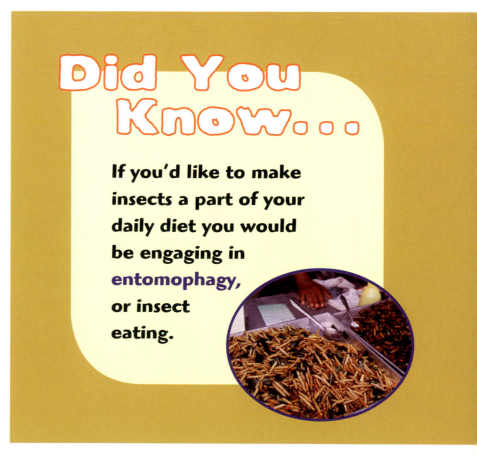

Did You Know...

If you'd like to make insects a part of your daily diet you would be engaging in **entomophagy**, or insect eating.

surround sound or one ounce of a bird's nest containing the saliva of an **Asian swiftlet**? Yes, for about the same price as a dream entertainment center, you could have this rare delicacy.

Certain kinds of swifts build nests in caves. Their nests are unusual because they are constructed from layers of dried saliva or spit. These homes look like cups and are stuck to the walls of caves. The nests are highly prized because they contain nutrients including iron, potassium, calcium and magnesium.

Since they are located high in remote caves, harvesting the nests is dangerous. Because the nests are worth so much money, greedy people take down so many of them that the birds cannot hatch their eggs. No hatched eggs, no more swifts. This makes the swift a bird that now needs protection to survive as a species.

Nests sell for $1,500 to $2,000 for one ounce. People use the nests for both soup and medicinal purposes. The nest is believed to be good for digestion, skin and lung conditions and certain reproductive problems. Blood red nests sell for the most money and there

Did You Know...

In January 2008 in Richmond, British Columbia, the Royal Canadian Mounted Police, better known as the Mounties, arrested three people for robbing a store of rare birds' nests. This marked the third robbery of such products over a short period of time in that city. Robberies like this are common occurrence in Hong Kong and Malaysia.

is a thriving business in making fake or counterfeit nests.

Bird's nest soup is one of the most expensive things you can eat, with a single bowl selling for $100!

A Meal To Die For

People don't eat things intentionally that will make them sick. Most meats, like chicken, hamburger and pork should be cooked to a high enough temperature to kill dangerous bacteria. But what about eating a dish that is so dangerous that even a small taste could kill you?

People in Japan eat **fugu** fish, which is one of the most famous or infamous dishes in this culture. Fugu can come from various sources of poisonous fish including the **putterfish,** and the **tiger blowfish.** These creatures have a natural poison in their liver and skin. This is not just any poison, it's **tetrodotoxin** and there's no cure once you've ingested it. Take a bite of this fish cut by an amateur sushi chef, and your mouth may start to feel funny. You feel queasy. You cannot move. You cannot breathe. And you are

wide awake as you die in a short period of time. If you can get to the hospital on time, you can be hooked up to a machine that will help you breathe and give you oxygen. If you don't die within

Fully "inflated" blowfish

"Deflated" poisonous Japanese pufferfish.

the first day, you might make it to eat fugu another day.

Because of the terrible risk of preparing this fish incorrectly, chefs are required to have special training and licenses before they're permitted to serve this dish. Even though most of this fish is consumed under the watchful eye of these experts, every year someone dies. It isn't easy becoming a certified chef and you must go to school for two to three years to learn this trade. You can expect to put your life on the line for about $50 for a serving.

Glossary

Algae – a simple plant-like organism, can be single celled or multicellular

Amputated – cut off, as when body parts are removed surgically

Anaesthetic – a drug used to cause the loss of sensation

Anal scent gland – an organ or specialized group of cells found in the anal region of many animals that give off an odorous chemical

Apocrine gland – a specialized group of cells under the skin that give off odorous chemicals

Bacteria – a group of microscopic creatures that lack chlorophyll, multiply by simple division, and are usually single-celled

Bile – a yellow-green or brown liquid given off by the liver

Bilirubin – a yellowish-red pigment found in human bile

Carnivorous – flesh-eating

Cerumen – secretory glands in the outer ear; the chemical given off by these glands

Cloaca – the cavity into which both the digestive and genital urinary systems empty in certain organism

Conjunctiva – the membrane lining the inner surface of the eyelids

Dermatophytes – plants that are skin parasites

Dung – feces

Entomophagy – the practice of eating insects

Enzymes – proteins that cause chemical changes to happen more quickly

Evisceration – to remove the internal organs

Feces – the waste material of the digestive system, excrement

Ferment – a breakdown of complex chemicals caused by yeast or bacteria

Fiber – slender thread-like structures

Flatulence – gas produced in the stomach or intestines

Fungus – a large group of organisms including mushrooms, yeasts, and molds that feed on organic materials, and reproduce by spores

Germs – a microscopic organism, such as a bacteria, that can cause disease

Gingivitis – inflammation of the gums

Glands – organs or groups of cells that produce fluids

Halitosis – bad breath

Herpetologist – a scientist who studies reptiles and amphibians

Host – an organism on or in which a parasite lives

Indole – a white crystalline chemical formed by the breakdown of proteins

Jacobson's organ – a chemical detecting organ found in the mouth of reptiles

Larva(e) – the early immature form of animals that change structure to become adults

Malassezia globosa – a tiny yeast-like fungus that can cause, dandruff and other skin conditions

Meconium – the greenish feces produced by newborn babies

Melanin – the pigment found in skin

Membrane – a thin flexible tissue or layer

Methane – a colorless, odorless, flammable gas, CH_4

Microfilariae – thin fibers containing reproductive material made by the loa loa worm

Mucoprotein – a type of protein found in mucous, plasma, gastric juices, and some other body fluids

Mucus – slimy mixture given off by the mucous membranes

Musk – a substance with a strong odor obtained from musk deer and some other animals

Neutrophils – a type of white blood cell

Nutrients – an ingredient in food which is good for you

Organism – any living thing

Organs – a body part made of specific types of cells that work together to have a particular function

Papillomaviruses – the viruses that cause warts

Paranoia – a mental health disorder

Parasite – a creature that gets its food and protection by living in or on another organism

Periodontist – a dentist who treats disorders of the gums and surrounding tissues

Pharyngeal Jaws – an extra set of jaws found in the throat region of the eel

Phlegm – mucus made in the respiratory system

Pineal body – a light sensitive organ on or in the head

Protozoa – a group of microscopic mostly single-celled organisms

Rheum – the watery discharge from the eye made from tears, mucus and other body fluids as well as dead skin cells and dust

Rostrum – the pointed beak of the assassin bug

Saliva – the fluid secreted by the salivary glands in the mouth

Sanguinivore – an organism that eats blood

Schizophrenia – a mental health disorder

Scolex – the head part of a tapeworm

Sensory hairs – tiny hair-like parts that stick out from carnivorous plants and that respond to touch

Skatole – a white crystalline chemical formed by the breakdown of proteins

Scent gland – a gland that releases a chemical with an odor

Symbiosis – a relationship between two species where both benefit

Slime mold – organisms that are often classified as a type of fungus but are sometimes considered to be a type of protozoa

Social amoeba – a protozoa that forms a social group or colony

Spadix – the spear-shaped organ of the corpse flower that contains the male and female flowers

Sphincter – a circular muscle like that of the anus

Spinnerets – the organ in spiders that spins thread for webs

Staph – an abbreviated name for the Staphylococcus aureus bacteria

Toxoplasmosis – a disease caused by protozoa that people can get from cats

Umbilical Cord – the tube that connects the navel of a fetus to its mother before birth

Urea – a very soluble chemical found in urine and other body fluids

Urohydrosis – the practice, common in vultures, of spreading feces on the body to cool it down

Venom – poison given off by some snakes, spiders, and insects

Zoonotic – a disease that can be transmitted to people by animals such as pets

---

Photo Credits

p. 11 Dog and hydrant photo copyright © Thinkstock/CORBIS

p. 33 Sunburned skin photo copyright © Richard Baker/CORBIS

p. 41 Water fleas photo copyright © Robert Pickett/CORBIS

p. 42 Piworms photo copyright © Lester V. Bergman/CORBIS

p. 43 Oesophagostumum Hookworm photo copyright © Lester V. Bergman/CORBIS

p. 44 Tapeworm image copyright © MedicalRF.com/CORBIS

p. 45 Schistosoma photo copyright © MedicalRF.com/CORBIS

p. 46 Leech photo copyright © Anthony Bannister; Gallo Images/CORBIS

p. 48 Amoeba photo copyright © Lester V. Bergman/CORBIS

p. 51 Zorilla photo copyright © Michael and Patricia Fogden/GettyImages

p. 59 Vampire bat photo copyright © Michael and Patricia Fogden/GettyImages

p. 61 Komodo Dragon photo copyright © Theo Allofs/CORBIS

p. 69 Mozambique Spitting Cobra photo copyright © Rod Patterson; Gallo Images/CORBIS

p. 70 Sonnoran Coral Snake photo copyright © Fotosearch

p. 73 Thornback ray photo copyright © JupiterImages

p. 74 Mosaic Moray Eel photo copyright © Tobias Bernhard/zefa/CORBIS

p. 77 Wrasse cleaning coral grouper photo copyright © Marty Snyderman/CORBIS

p. 80 Archer fish photo copyright © DK Limited/CORBIS

p. 100 Corpse flower (Titan Arum) photo copyright © Pawel Libera/CORBIS

p. 107 Civet photo (top) copyright © Reuters/CORBIS; Edible bugs photo (bottom) copyright © Madcuff Everton/CORBIS

All other images courtesy of iStockphoto

Index

A

Abscess, 26
Acne, 31–32
Alcon blue butterfly, 89
Aldrovandaare, 98
Algae, on two-toed sloths, 57
Alkaloids, 84
Ambergris, 3
Amoeba, 48
Amoebic dysentery, 48
Amphibians, 62–65. *See also* Frogs
    baby toads popping off mom's back, 63–64
    deadly toads, 62–63
    "eye" in back of head, 64–65
    eyes helping swallow food, 65
    tadpoles growing in dad's mouth, 64
Amylase, 22
Anal scent glands, 50
Animals. *See also* Ocean life; Reptiles
    awful amphibians, 62–65. See also Frogs
    revolting diets of, 58–61
    that smell bad. See Odiferous animals
    that spread things on themselves, 56–57
Anosmia, 47
Antarctic icefish, 76
Anteaters, 58–59
Apocrine glands, 15–16
Archer fish, 79–80
Ascariasis, 42
Ascaris lumbricoides, 42
Asian swiftlet, eating saliva of, 108–109
Assassin bugs, 87
Athlete's foot, 29

B

Bacteria
    bad breath and, 20
    body odor and, 15–16
    in carnivorous plants, 95
    in cheese, 102
    in eyes (causing styes), 36
    in feces, 8
    foot odor and, 27–28
    killing, to make food safe, 109
    process of body eliminating, 33–34
    pus and, 33–34
    in saliva, 22–23
    tooth decay and gum disease from, 24–26
Bad breath, 20
Bats, vampire, 59–60
Belly button lint, 18
Belly buttons, 18
Benzoquinones, 84
Bile, 3

Bilirubin, 7
Bird's nest soup, 108–109
Blood
    in diarrhea, 48
    leeches sucking, 45–46
    vampire bats drinking, 59–60
    in vomit, 3
Blood pressure, lizard changing, 63
Body odor. *See* Sweat
Boogers, boogies, bogies, 5
Breath, bad, 20
Brevibacterium linens, 102
Bugs, 81–92
    assassinating prey, 87
    chemical mimicry of, 89
    eating insects, 105–106, 107
    eating insect vomit, 105
    spiders and webs, 85–86
    stinky, 82–84
    taking control of host's mind, 88
    taking over snail tentacles, 89
    walking up walls, on ceilings, 86
Bunga bangkai, 99–100
Butterwort, 96

C

Canadian wood frog, 76
Cane toads, 62–63
Carnivorous plants. *See* Plants, carnivorous
Centipedes, 84
Cerumen, 19
Cheese
    feet smelling like, 28–29
    smelly, 29, 102–104
Chemical mimicry, 89
Chromhidrosis, 17
Civets, 54, 106–107
Cleaner fish, 76–77
Cleaning symbiosis, 77
Cloacal popping, 70
Coast horned lizards, 63
Coffee, from civet poop, 106–107
Colds, mucus and, 6
Colds, mucus/saliva and, 23
Conjunctiva, 35–36
Corals, 91–92
Corps (cadaver) flower, 99
Cradle cap, 30
Crap. *See* Feces (poop)

D

Dandruff (scurf), 30–31
Darwin frog, 64
Dentin, 24. *See also* Teeth
Dermatophytes, 29
Diarrhea, 9, 48
Digestion. *See also* Food